Fun with American History

E. Richard & Linda R.
CHURCHILL
Edward H.
BLAIR

Fun with American History

ABINGDON PRESS (AP) New York • Nashville

FUN WITH AMERICAN HISTORY

Copyright © 1966 by Abingdon Press

Library of Congress Catalog Card Number: 66-10849

SET UP, PRINTED, AND BOUND BY THE
PARTHENON PRESS, AT NASHVILLE,
TENNESSEE, UNITED STATES OF AMERICA

To

    Dr. Arthur R. Reynolds
    Chairman, Department of Social Sciences
    Colorado State College
    Greeley, Colorado

        and

To the Memory of

    Dr. John S. Welling
    Professor of Social Studies
    Colorado State College
    Greeley, Colorado

Preface

The authors firmly believe that book introductions should be either extremely interesting or very short. We'll settle for shortness and hope for the best.

Here is a book for people of all ages who are interested in the United States, its history, people, and geography. It will review former learning and provide new adventures in knowledge.

A generous selection of games and activities open the book. The quizzes and puzzles which follow may be used in conjunction with the games or by themselves. Play may begin at any point in the book. Our cross-references will refer the player to related activities and quiz answers; so skip around as much as you wish with no fear of getting lost.

We have tried to hit all major areas of American history and geography, but have especially picked up little known and interesting material which seldom appears in the classroom. The book provides all players with a starting point—we haven't said it all. When you find an area of interest, go ahead on your own. You will be learning and having fun at the same time.

Use our book for individual fun, family fun, party fun, and school fun. It has many uses in many places.

Paper and pencil are all the players need to go with the book, though an inquiring mind is a big asset. We would suggest that players not write in the book.

Now let's have the book speak for itself. Turn the page and hang on to your hat, for America is a great country with a fascinating history. It is not all within the covers of this book, but enough of our heritage is here to give you many hours of challenging and educational entertainment.

E. Richard and Linda R. Churchill
Edward H. Blair

Contents

Quizzes from History

Geographical Quizzes

Games
and
Activities

Ballads from History

Here is an activity which can be an excellent end of the evening activity when the group is in the mood for something of interest but not interested in competition with one another.

Pick a simple melody of a well-known old favorite song and make sure that everybody is familiar with the tune. Then, working individually or in groups, compose a folk song or ballad about an event in history. The climax to the game comes with the singing of the ballads (or reciting them if the players desire) to the rest of the group. Here a piano is a great asset to the activity. Who knows but what some ballad written in this manner might make its way onto the American musical scene at some future date?

Try the "Ballad of Bunker Hill" or the "Ballad of Bull Run" as starting ideas and work from there. Of course this activity may be modified to become a game of composing narrative poetry without regard to composing a ballad if the players wish, though the ballads are apt to be a bit more interesting when sung to the group.

Be Conversant

In this interesting game two players (more if necessary) decide upon two related characters from American history and talk to each other for a minute or so, pretending they are the characters they have selected. As they talk, they drop clues to their identity so that other players may eventually guess their identities. If the other players are unable to correctly give the names of the persons impersonated, the conversationalists converse again, being more obvious in their talking as to their chosen identities.

This game provides a way of adding to the information players have concerning famous people as well as improving listening skills. An exciting review of historic events and great biographical characters comes naturally while giving free reign to the development and exercise of dramatic talents.

The player correctly identifying the conversationalists may choose a partner and become the next person to converse, or the turn may rotate around the group as is desired.

As starters the group might use Lewis and Clark, Grant and Lee, or Sutter and Marshall.

Categorically Speaking

Many of our best known quiz games for play at home or for listening and viewing on radio and television involve the use of specific categories which change with every question. Here is one in that tradition.

The opening player gives the group a category, such as a city in Colorado. The first to call out the correct answer gains a point and the right to select the next category which might be an American general from World War II. This might be followed by a President before 1900 and so on, keeping the group constantly alert and hoping for a question which isn't too rough.

Here is one for the person who has looked high and low for a game which never grows old. You may wish to limit your categories to history, geography, or biography, or to allow any category. The choice of limiting categories is up to the group; but whether you choose to restrict categories or not, we are sure you will enjoy this fast moving quiz game more every time you play it.

Changing History

Here is a chance to change history by merely using your wits and a sharp pencil. The object is to change a word pertaining to history to another word which also pertains to history. If possible, it is fun to change a word to another word having an opposite meaning, or to a word which relates to the beginning word. You are allowed to change one letter at a time but each change must form a new word.

Basically, you are constructing a list of words in which the word before and after each word is like that word except for a difference of one letter. This test of wits and determination is great for spare minutes of time. When players have constructed a list of these words, exchange them and have other members of the group attempt to make the necessary changes. It is often a real feat of mental endurance to accomplish the task.

As a starter, why not try to change "bond" to "free." You should be able to do it in nine changes or less.

Here is a possible solution: bond, Gond (look it up if you don't believe us!), goad, goat, boat, beat, beet, feet, fret, free.

Coded Quotations

There is probably no more fascinating activity than that of constructing codes and decoding material set up by other persons. These codes may be made by substituting one letter for another, substituting numerals for letters, inventing symbols for letters, or any of a dozen ways players might devise.

The coding of famous quotations can be lots of fun as well

as informative. It will come as a surprise to many players to discover upon checking their quotation in a collection that many of our most famous quotations are either misquoted or attributed to the wrong person. That, however, is just part of the interest this game arouses.

Writing of codes is usually as much fun as the decoding of someone else's coded quotation. In setting up codes for fellow players to decode be doubly sure that your code is correct. Don't slip in two symbols for the same letter. It is easily done and makes decoding difficult.

When the time for decoding arrives, begin by looking for one and two letter words in the quotation. These will be your best clues and will usually get you on the road to success. Another aid to decoding will be the name of the author of the quotation, which is written below the last line in the statement. After having discovered several letters, it is often possible to identify the author's name, giving you many additional letters to fill into your coded message. Shrewd deduction, determined thinking, and luck will be needed to carry you to success in this game.

Code makers may give clues as to the identity of a letter or two if the decoders get bogged down, but don't give up too easily on this activity.

As a contest activity this is really tops. Have the players provide a coded quotation each, exchange quotations, and the race is on. The first player to correctly decode the quotation given him is the winner. Everyone wants another chance because they have a great idea for a code for the next quotation.

On pages 101 and 103, you will find a few quotations we have set in code for you. Better give them a try right now and see how good you are at solving our codes.

Crosswords and Criss-Crosses

Constructing a crossword puzzle is probably the only thing more fascinating than solving one. Building and solving cross-

and crisscross puzzles can turn a group activity into a
rable occasion. Puzzle building becomes even more fun
eme is selected for the puzzle and followed as closely as
le. Building a puzzle of American military heroes is far
more challenging and educational than merely constructing an
ordinary crossword puzzle. Of course any such puzzle will include many words not related to the main theme, but players
will be surprised at how easily many words related to a given
theme can be worked into a puzzle.

For most groups, depending upon age and experience, one
of the following three puzzle types will prove superior to the
formal puzzle found in the evening paper.

The first illustration below suggests a puzzle which may be
built either horizontally or vertically by the younger set. It
goes only one way with no attempt to cross words within the
puzzle. Concentrate on good clues and follow the main theme
in the puzzle; then watch the young puzzle builders go.

A word chain or criss-cross is the idea behind the second
illustration. Beginners will want to make the word chain as
shown at the beginning of the puzzle, and more advanced puzzle
makers will be challenged by the criss-cross which begins at the
end of the puzzle. Such a puzzle builds up and down across
the paper with as many twists, turns, and crossings as the puzzle
builder can work into his puzzle. Again the emphasis is on good
clues and sticking to a theme from history.

Before building one of your own, you will enjoy working one
or more of our criss-crosses and box puzzles found on pages
52, 72, 143, 153, and 179.

A more conventional puzzle type is seen in the last illustration. Again, stress the idea of good clues and trying to use related
words whenever possible. Don't worry about making a balanced
puzzle. Just block out the square at the end of each word and
have fun building your puzzle.

Building these puzzles is great for those odd minutes of time when nothing else seems to be a good idea. Encourage players to build and collect these puzzles for challenge matches with other players.

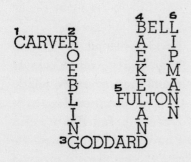

This little puzzle had as its theme "Western explorers" as may be seen from the completed example. Its clues might be:

1. When exploring the Louisiana Purchase, this military man failed to climb a mountain which bears his name.
2. This scout once guided Frémont through the Rockies. (3, 4, and 5 in like manner.)

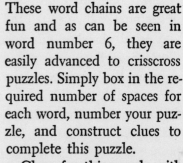

These word chains are great fun and as can be seen in word number 6, they are easily advanced to crisscross puzzles. Simply box in the required number of spaces for each word, number your puzzle, and construct clues to complete this puzzle.

Clues for this puzzle with the theme of "Scientists and Inventors" might go:

Across

1. Man engaged in agricultural research at Tuskegee Institute
3. Rocket scientist

Down

2. Noted inventor in area of steel and bridge work
4. Noted inventor of photo paper (And so on through the length of the puzzle.)

¹G	²R	³A	N	⁴T
⁵L	E	T	▓	E
⁶O	D	E	⁷T	S
R	▓	▓	⁸E	L
Y	▓	⁹A	A	A

This puzzle (which can be made as large or as small as the puzzle builder wishes) used "American history" as its theme.

The following clues might be used:

Across

1. Union general defeating Lee
5. To allow

Down

1. America's flag is often called Old _____.
2. During the Colonial era British troops were called _____ coats. (And so on.)

Date Time

This one should make a hit with the history buffs. It requires that the players either know or learn something about the dates in history.

The leader, whose job passes around the group after each contest, gives the players the name of a month, year, decade, historic era, or perhaps a century. He then counts to ten at a moderate rate. When he reaches the end of his counting, he starts around the group asking each player in turn to give an event which occurred during the period of time he named. Each player correctly supplying an event earns a point. Each player who is unable to give an event or who gives an event already mentioned by a player receives no point for his efforts; instead, the point goes to the leader.

It is best to begin this game giving broad periods of time such as a century, a decade, or perhaps an era such as the Colonial Period so that players have a fairly wide choice of events. As the players become better acquainted with the game, begin to narrow the categories down into given years. When the category of months is used, any event which occurred in the month given from any year is a correct answer. Real history buffs may, however, wish to give categories such as April, 1945, in which case only events from that particular month would be used.

Disguises

When the group needs a bit of mental stimulation, this game should provide a ready answer. Its object is to disguise the name of a city, state, river, geographical feature, or a famous person within a reasonable sentence. The disguised word may be hidden within a longer word or broken up among two or more words. The only rule which must not be broken is that the letters of the disguised name follow each other in correct order, with no other letters appearing among those spelling the hidden word. Thus when the disguised word is finally located, it is spelled correctly though it may be broken into numerous parts.

As players construct sentences containing disguised names, they may present their written creations to the rest of the group so that they may attempt to uncover the word. One player's sentences may be presented at a time, or the contributions of all the players may be jumbled together and presented in mass. This game works well with a time limit or with the person first discovering a disguised word being awarded a point. Decide how your group wants to play the game; but play it, for it is great fun and a real thought encourager.

Here is a sample just to make sure you have the idea:

"Are Bess and I egotists?"

The city of San Diego is disguised in the example just in case you had a bit of trouble locating it.

Now that you have the idea, get going on some disguises of your own. You may want to give the group a clue as to the identity of the word they are hunting if they get stuck on an especially difficult disguise.

On pages 113 and 169, you will find some quizzes we have

prepared along the same lines as in the above example. Give them a try before going on to another game.

Familiar Faces

A bit of preparation goes into this game, but the game is well worth the effort. Pictures of well-known people of the present and past are collected from newspapers and magazines and mounted on fairly stiff paper.

The players are challenged to identify the pictures. This identification may be carried out in a variety of ways. Perhaps the players will be asked to name the person. They might be called upon to give the person's country, achievements, time in history, or any number of other interesting items. For variety why not present two pictures and ask which, if either, of the two is living? You might also display two or more pictures and ask in what way or ways the people portrayed are related or alike.

Each group will devise additional ways of playing the game as well as how to score the responses. It works well as a game of elimination or as a high-point game.

As a test of facial recognition and association this game rates at the top of the list. As an attention and interest getter it is also high on the ladder. You will be surprised at the variety of ways in which the activity may be used and the responses which will come from a group when confronted with a well-chosen series of portraits.

Geographical Scrambles

The leader or first player in line chooses a geographical name and scrambles the letters. He presents it to the group for unscrambling. The first player to correctly unscramble the word receives a point for his efforts, and the turn to scramble a word passes to the player at the right of the first scrambler. This continues until all players have had the same number of turns at scrambling geographical words and terms.

It is a good idea, at least at first, to set categories for each game and limit scrambles to words from within the selected category. When you know that all scrambles are state names, for instance, it is not nearly so difficult to identify lradooooc as Colorado.

Preparing lists of scrambles and exchanging them among players, instead of giving the group one word at a time with which to work, provides for increased interest in this game.

Setting up categories from history and biography can also add to the fun of the activity. In fact, it is limited only by the imaginations of the players and the time at their disposal.

Geography

Quick thinking and a good knowledge of geographical names and locations have their place in this game for quick-witted geography students. The leader begins the game by giving the name of a place. The second player continues the game by giving the name of a place beginning with the letter with which the first name ended. This continues around the group until a player cannot supply the name of a city, river, mountain, or other place in his turn. He drops out of play; the next in line takes the letter which caused his downfall, and the game continues until only one player remains and is declared winner.

The game might run in this fashion:

First player: "New York"

Second player: "Kansas City"

Third player: "Yuma"

Fourth and all other players continue in like manner.

An excellent variation of this game is to require each player to contribute a fact about the name he gives. This may be a fact of history or of a geographical nature, so long as it pertains to the name of the given place. Thus, this game not only provides a learning experience in geography, but an additional review of the history of certain places.

Guggenheim

Here is a brain tickler which provides an interesting review of geography, history, and biography while challenging players to the utmost. Besides all this, it is great fun.

Each player has his own playing sheet which he rules into a column labeled "Category" and one column for each letter of the four- or five-letter starter word given by the leader. When the game begins, the object is to supply a word for each category beginning with each letter of the starter word. Thus, if you set up five categories and the starter word has four letters, a total of twenty words is required to complete the playing sheet.

Each player works to complete his sheet within the set time limit (usually ten minutes). Each space filled correctly gives a player five points, while each space left blank at the end of the time limit takes ten points from the total score.

Each new game uses a new starter word, and if desired new categories may be supplied. Though four- or five-letter starter words are usually used, there is no reason why longer or shorter words cannot be used if a longer or shorter game is desired. Of course the number of categories may also be changed as the group wishes. Six categories may become four or eight or any other number. Again, this is up to the group. Allowing group members to name a category at a time in rotation adds to the interest and lets players slip in favorite categories.

The example should make clear any questions concerning this game.

It is interesting to note that many famous people play and enjoy this fascinating game. Perhaps the most famous player in recent years was President John F. Kennedy, who is said to have greatly enjoyed this game.

Starting word: work

27

Category	W	O	R	K
General	Wallace			
President	Wilson			
Battle				King's Mt.
State		Oregon		Kansas
River			Red	
City		Omaha		

Historic Affinities

Affinities, as you probably already know, are things which go together like salt and pepper, ham and eggs, or time and tide.

Just a little thought will call to mind many cases of affinities in history. For instance, George and Martha come at once to mind as representatives from the Revolutionary era in U.S. history, while Burns and Allen come to us from the very recent past.

Have the players compile lists of such affinities or use the game as a contest of elimination in which every player supplies an affinity in turn or quits the group. It is also lots of fun to have a player give his affinity and then give half of an affinity to the next player who must supply the missing half to stay in the game. He, of course, would give the next in line half of a new affinity and so on down the line. In the event a player is forced to drop out, the next player must take the affinity which proved a stumper and deal with it himself. When played this way, a player who can't supply a starter for the next in line pays the penalty by being eliminated from play.

Before you have played the game many times, you should turn to page 129 and tackle the pairs we have assembled there.

Historic Charades

At one time or another everyone has played the game of "Charades." This game allows for individual dramatic display or for team acting. Its object is simple. A person or group decide upon a character, group of characters, or an event from history which they wish to portray for the rest of the group. They quickly act out a skit of the event for the others. As soon as a viewer can identify the person or event being depicted, he calls out his answer. If he is right, he gains a point and the right to participate in the next historic charade. If he is incorrect in his guess, the action continues, and others try their luck.

Should no one correctly guess the idea behind the action, the actors may either repeat their performance or continue it until a correct guess comes forth. Should they have a person in mind, it is a good idea to act out another event in his life so that the viewers may get another slant on things.

It may be a good idea for each actor or group of actors to tell the group at the beginning of the charade whether they have a character or an event in mind. This, however, is up to the group.

Try this game, and you'll be surprised how many half-forgotten events from history come to mind as perfect ideas for a historic charade, making this an excellent activity to keep in mind for a return engagement.

With groups of fairly young children (elementary age, perhaps), this activity may be of more interest and fun if performed in the manner of a television show. A little preparation may be desired in this case, and a fairly polished performance may develop. Let several groups prepare their performances in various parts of the room. Then have each present their creation to the others who in turn get to give their presentation as soon as they can guess the theme of the group on stage. This activity is fine for the would-be actors in the group and also provides an interesting history lesson as the groups plan their charades so that they are historically correct.

Historical Fill-Ins

Here is a quickie designed to occupy a group for a few minutes of contest fun. It can be used again at later dates.

A category is chosen, such as the Civil War, and each player prepares a list of ten words or so pertaining to the chosen category. When each player has completed his lists, papers are exchanged and the fun begins. When the words in the list were written, they were written with only three letters. Blanks represent missing letters. Thus Lincoln (Civil War category) might appear as _ _ n c _ l _. The first player to completely fill in the blanks with no errors wins the event. If the task gets too rugged, a time limit may be set with the winner being the individual having the most words correctly completed.

It may be a good idea to require the first, last, and one middle letter to be written by all players in preparing their fill-ins. Or perhaps the players might write only the final three letters of all words, and so on for many interesting variations.

Don't forget the possibility of using this game in the areas of geography and biography as well as history. The category of famous American women can be lots of fun and educational for the males in the group.

Play the game with any dozens of variations and categories, and you will find yourself returning to it again and again when you need a quick contest with high interest.

History on Trial

For a different history game try setting up a court scene and trying a case from history. A presiding judge keeps order, and this should nearly always be the job of an adult or mature youngster. A jury is necessary, though it need not contain twelve members. Attorneys for both defense and prosecution play important parts as do the defendant and all witnesses called.

Such a trial may be as simple or as involved as the participants desire, with little or much preparation going into the activity. The judge decides how much leeway to allow the attorneys in the questioning of witnesses. Some attorneys will prove to be experts at cross-examination and may have to be checked at times, should they prove a bit too rough on the witnesses, though good attorneys make this activity even more interesting than do clever witnesses.

Don't worry about formality; instead, rely on the imagination of the participants and what everyone has seen on television to get this activity off to a good beginning.

As suggestions you might wish to try George Washington for chopping down his father's cherry tree, Paul Revere for beating his horse during his famous ride, the "Indians" who took part in the Boston Tea Party, or Theodore Roosevelt for his actions against Panama.

Cases tried may be of a serious or lighthearted nature, depending upon the group playing the game. Just remember to decide on witnesses before the game begins so that they may have a moment or two to prepare their accounts. Invent witnesses, allow attorneys to give witnesses brief facts concerning what they "saw," let the defendant choose a witness in his behalf, and let players volunteer to be witnesses and make up their facts as they go.

This game can be great fun and turn into a comedy or may be strictly factual with all questions and answers played according to history. Either way, it is a splendid activity.

I'm a Historian

The first player begins this game by stating, "I'm a historian, and I write about. . . ." He goes on to tell what he writes about. Should he decide to write about Indians, the next person would continue, "I'm a historian, and I write about Samoset." (Any Indian would do, of course.) Each player in turn continues the game, except that he gives the name of a famous Indian not already mentioned. Those who can't give a name are dropped, and the game goes on. Should any player feel that a "historian" doesn't really know what he is talking about, he may challenge him to give a fact about the person named. If he can't, he is forced to drop; but if he is successful, the person challenging drops from the game. Last player in the circle wins, as might be expected.

For a tougher variation better suited to the older players, try the same game except that each item given must begin with the ending letter of the previous name given. Samoset might be followed by Tecumseh, for instance.

Here is a good game which is apt to start fast and end quickly unless the players are up on their facts and personages.

I'm Thinking of a Person

This one is especially for the younger historians, though adults may find it rough when a real history buff is "thinking of a person."

The game begins with a player telling the group, "I'm thinking of a person whose name begins with. . . ." He gives them the letter with which the person's last name begins. After a few incorrect guesses (say three) he allows a question concerning the identity of the person. This he answers and then allows three more guesses. This continues until a player identifies the unknown person and becomes the leader for the next game.

The game may be varied by having the leader give a fact after every few guesses instead of answering questions put to him.

As we said, this is great fun for the elementary age players, but watch the adults stumble when they have to identify an individual whose name begins with W and that person happens to be William Wirt of 1832 election fame.

Lives of the Great

Players who do not know many facts concerning the lives of great and interesting Americans will soon remedy that situation when they play this game.

The leader decides upon a person whose fame is well established in America. He then gives the group ten facts about the life of that person. He gives these facts one at a time, allowing for one guess per player after each fact is presented. Should a player guess after the first clue the individual the leader had in mind, that player gets ten points toward his total score. A correct identification after the second clue rates nine points, after the third fact eight points, and on down to an award of one point should the person be guessed after the tenth and last clue. Should no player guess the person the leader has in mind, the leader gets ten points.

The opportunity to be leader rotates around the group so that everyone gets to lead. Some groups play until they wish to change games and declare the player with the highest total of points winner at that time. Many people, however, prefer to set a point at which the game ends. Perhaps twenty-five points for one player would end the game with that player winning. This score may be altered to fit the size of the group and the time available for play. The larger the group, the harder it is for one player to gain a high score; so don't set too high a total the first time through this game.

Mapping Your Way

Road maps are free and provide the basis for many educational and fascinating games and activities. The reader might try the suggestions which follow and then strike out on his own in inventing ways of having fun while learning the use of road maps.

In the first activity begin by cutting off the locator guide or by folding it under the rest of the map. A player gives the name of a place found on the map and times his fellow player or players while they attempt to locate the place. (If more than two people play, each player should be supplied with his own map.) Play then alternates between players or rotates around the group if more than two play. The winner at the end of each round of play is the one who locates the place given in the shortest elapsed time, or the player who first located the given place when a group is taking part in the contest. The game may be varied by using maps of different states and is a good one to return to again.

A second idea is to assign the players a trip to take on their maps. They may travel between two points of interest, or there may be as many as a dozen points through which they must travel. The winner may be the player who completes his trip first, or it may be the person who completes his journey in the shortest number of miles. A written record may be kept by outlining the trip on the map with a pencil or by recording mileage, places seen, and highway routes on another sheet of paper. Either way, it aids map reading, exposes the players to the geography of an area, and is loads of fun.

A third variation of map fun is to assign the players a given number of miles to travel and have as an objective the seeing of the greatest number of towns, landmarks, and points of interest. The winner will be the player who plans ahead and plots his course with an eye to the future.

Opportunities for fun and learning via the road map are countless and never ending. Use them once, and you will find yourself using them again as new and varied game and contest ideas present themselves.

My Friend Was There

Players had best keep their wits about them in this fast moving quiz game, or they may be left in the lurch while their faster thinking opponents surge on to victory.

A player tells the group, "My friend was a general at the Battle of B.H." The first player to call out the words represented by the initials <u>B.H.</u> receives a point and gives the next "My friend" statement to the group.

This game can gather speed at an alarming rate and can get

really tough. Remember that generals and privates seldom engage in sea battles, though admirals and seamen do. There is no ruling that items chosen must use two initials, though some groups prefer to set some such limit. It is usually cumbersome, however, to allow the use of over three initials in a clue.

The game is not limited to battles, though it is often fun to set categories for several turns and then give new categories to work with.

If a player stumps the others, give him a point and have the player to his right give the next "My friend" statement.

Name the States

This little test of memory is designed to fill a few minutes with a good mental exercise. It may be returned to again and again without becoming stale and has a dozen possible variations of the main theme. What's more, it can be good fun as well.

Basically, this game is a naming contest in which the players attempt to name all the states beginning with a given letter before continuing to another letter. For instance, the leader may ask for all the states whose names begin with the letter M. The player to first complete his list wins the point and gives the starting letter for the next list.

Perhaps the group wishes to play the game in rotation; if so, the leader asks for the letter M, and the next player in line gives a state beginning with that letter and immediately gives a letter for the next player. This continues until a player is unable to give a state name of the letter assigned him and is forced to drop from play. By using a no-repeat rule this game can get rugged in a short time. If a player assigns another a letter which is impossible, because no states begin with that letter or all the states have been named beginning with that letter, that player is forced to drop from the game should he be challenged. If a player is challenged and can supply a correct answer, however, the challenger is dropped from play.

As the game is played, countless variations will present themselves. Using state capitals instead of state names adds to the fun and makes for a much tougher game.

Nicknames

The learning of the nicknames of the states of the American nation can prove to be an interesting and educational activity. Once begun, it is not long until members of the group have learned the nicknames of all fifty of the states. Learning these nicknames leads to a study of history and geography when one attempts to discover how a nickname came into being. Thus, this activity contributes to several areas of learning while providing for family and group fun.

This activity may be used as a listing game in which all players attempt to list as many states and their nicknames as possible within a given time limit. It also works well when played as a group game of rotation in which each player in his turn names a state and its nickname. Players who have a correct combination score a point, or those having an incorrect response are eliminated from the game. In the first case the player having the highest score is winner, while in the second instance the last remaining player wins. When the game is played in rotation, why not let each player supply the next with either a state or nickname to be correctly matched?

You might like to look at page 172, where we have a nickname quiz for you which will get you started with this game.

This game also proves to be a lot of fun when used with the nicknames given to noted people. Page 127 will get you off to a good start with some nicknames we have included for your attention.

Quiz Football

Don't let the fact that a player knows next to nothing about the game of football stop you for a minute on this game. The rules we have here will take care of that failing within minutes.

A playing field is necessary. The quickest way to make this field is to number a sheet of lined paper in the manner of a football field. The center line is marked as fifty, and the lines on either side are marked forty-five, forty, thirty-five, and so forth until the zero or goal line is reached near the top and near the bottom of the paper. A marker to represent the ball is needed; so better locate something small (a paper clip is best since it is clipped to the paper and slides along the edge nicely as the play moves up and down the field). Now you are ready to play.

Questions for this game may come from the quiz section of this book or from the players themselves. A team may be of any size, though teams are best kept small. If the group is fairly large, use small teams and have several games going at once so that a tournament may be played.

A flip of a coin or any other desired method decides which team will first carry the ball. They receive the ball on their own twenty-yard line which gives them eighty yards to go for a touchdown.

The defending team (the one without the ball) begins play by asking a quiz question. The team with the ball must answer the questions asked them in order to advance down the field. As in regular football four plays (questions) are allowed a team when it has possession of the ball. Each correct answer advances the ball five yards; each missed question causes a loss of five yards. If you advance ten yards in your turn from the point at which your team took control of the ball, you start anew with four more questions.

Any time a team takes possession of the ball and is able to advance within thirty yards of the opponents' goal line by the first or second down, they may—if they wish—attempt a field goal for a possible three points. In this case they state their intentions and are given three questions which they must answer correctly in order to score. Should they miss any question of the three, the other team takes over the ball at the point where it was when the goal was attempted.

When one team crosses the other team's goal line, it receives six points for the goal and a chance for the extra point or points after the goal. The scoring team may choose to attempt a one- or two-point play at this time. They are given either one or two questions for this attempt. Correct answers give them either their one or two points; but if a two-point play is attempted, both questions must be answered correctly in order to score.

After each goal, whether a field goal or a rushing goal, the team scored against takes the ball on their own twenty-yard line as in the beginning of the game, and play resumes.

Should a team be forced back over their own goal line, because of missed questions when they are carrying the ball, their foes gain two points and possession of the ball on their own twenty-yard line as at the game's beginning. Time limits are good, as are games which end when one side achieves a given score.

This game is exceptionally good for sports-minded youngsters but is fun for players of all ages. Questions may cover any area of history or geography desired and may be as difficult or as easy as the skill of the players permits.

Quiz Golf

Using the idea of golf scoring adds a lot of fun and excitement to group quizzes on history, geography, or any related areas. Each player numbers his score sheet from one to nine or from one to eighteen depending on how many holes the group decides to play.

The leader gives a question to the first player who attempts to give the correct answer to the question. If he answers the question correctly on his first attempt, he records his score for the hole, which is one stroke. If he is incorrect in his answer, however, he records a stroke and again attempts to answer the question. This continues until he answers the question correctly or until he has missed the question four times. In this event he records a fifth penalty stroke, and the same question is given to the next player.

If the preceding player misses his question four times, it is passed to the next player; but if he answers his question, the next player is, of course, given a new question. The quiz continues in this manner until all the players have played their nine or eighteen <u>holes</u>. Each player keeps his own score of one stroke per answer and a penalty stroke on the fourth wrong answer to a given question.

If a question stumps all the players, the leader answers it for them rather than starting it on a second round.

At the end of the game the player having the lowest total score is declared winner and becomes the leader for the next game.

This challenging game may be played using prepared quizzes such as those found within this book or questions given by the leader. It also works nicely to have each player prepare a list of questions and answers which the leader uses in playing the game. When a player gets his own question, he is sure of a one-stroke <u>hole</u>, which just adds to the fun and excitement of the game.

Rhymes

Here is one for the rapid thinker which is based upon rhymes. Each player in turn gives the group a clue in rhyme concerning the name of a person, event, or place in history. For instance, the opening player might tell the group, "I'm thinking of a Civil War general whose name rhymes with bee." The first player to supply the correct answer (Lee) receives a point. If a player in his turn is unable to supply a rhyme, he loses a point from his score. Each correct answer to another's rhyme nets him a point.

Players may choose any category they wish from history and may use their imagination in achieving a rhyme. For example, a player might rhyme "tacks on" with "Jackson" and be perfectly happy in his rhyme. Should a player pose a stumper for the group, give him two points as a reward for his cleverness.

This game may be used quite handily with geographical places as well as with historic items.

Search Them Out

Players of all ages will tackle this game again and again with delight, as it never grows old and is always a new game whenever it is played. The object is to locate words hidden within a longer word or phrase.

The leader begins by choosing a word from history which has eight or more letters, though the longer the word, the more interesting the game becomes. The players, leader included, then begin the exciting search for smaller words which may be formed using only the letters found within the starter word or phrase. Should the starter word contain a letter more than once, this letter may be used one time or as many times as it appears in the starter word in any word formed by the players.

Any word which may be spelled by using only letters from the starter word gives the player spelling it a point. Any word having to do with history carries a bonus of an extra point for its discoverer. Better set rules concerning the use of abbreviations, nicknames, musical syllables, and the like before beginning the game. It is important to remember that the letters used to spell smaller words do not need to be used in the same order as they appear in the starter word—they need only appear in the starter word.

This is a good time limit game, an excellent group project, or an extended project to return to during spare moments.

It may also be used with biographical names and geographical place names. When it is used with famous people, award bonus points for words relating to the life and achievements of the person whose name was used as a starter word. Words relating to the geographical name used would rate as bonus words in that contest.

After having done a few of these on your own, turn to pages 151 and 152, and try your hand at the word searches we have prepared for you.

Speak Your Piece

It never fails to surprise a group of people to find just how difficult it is to talk steadily about a given subject for thirty seconds, especially when that subject is an event in history about which the player has merely foggy memories about names and dates.

The idea of this little contest is simple, but its accomplishment is difficult, if not impossible for many. Players are assigned a subject from history on which to speak without interruption for thirty seconds. Of course it would be considered extremely poor taste to repeat oneself or mumble during the speech. The game may be played with players in the group taking turns speaking or with two speakers facing each other and talking about the same subject. Decide who the winning speaker is by either judging the content of the oration or by the simple method of declaring the only player to finish without hesitation as the winner. No matter how the contest is judged, the younger members of the family are apt to carry away all honors.

Try such subjects as "I saw Pickett charge," "I was a friend of Major André," or "I rode Comanche into the Battle of the Little Big Horn," and watch the would-be speakers melt like butter. The game can be played as straight history or in a light-hearted fashion, as the group desires. Either way is bound to keep the group on its collective toes.

There's a State in That Song

For a quick check on song favorites of past and present, as well as a quiz on state names, this game goes to the head of the list.

41

It is a listing or rotation contest involving the names of songs which contain state names. Each player compiles a list of as many song titles (in which state names appear) as he can within a given time limit. A good variation of this idea is to have the players compile lists of the song titles containing the name of a given state, which is a much harder, though a shorter contest since each state is a game in itself. And, of course, this game is one of the many which adapts wonderfully to use as an elimination contest wherein each player must supply a title or drop from play.

Don't overlook the use of river names, names of cities, lake names, or names of mountains when playing this game.

Perhaps even more interesting than the game itself are the memories called to mind by the song titles which are used in the game. Should the game eventually change from a naming game to a song fest, who really minds?

You might wish to vary this game somewhat by using song titles which contain the names of people or events from history such as "John Henry" and the like. You will be surprised at the number of folk songs and ballads a group can call to mind which fit into this classification.

Three for a Story

Here is an outstanding activity especially designed for the younger members. It provides them with an opportunity to create and entertain by using their imagination in storytelling.

The group member chosen to be the storyteller is given three items of historic significance by three members of the group. It is best that these items be as unrelated and unlike as possible to challenge the storyteller. As soon as the three suggested items have been given him, the storyteller at once begins telling his story, which must logically include the three things suggested to him. Youngsters will seldom fail to include the three items in an interesting story, but the test of the storyteller's magic comes in making the story historically sound as well as interesting.

When the storyteller has completed his story, another player takes up the task of storyteller, is presented with three items from history, and the round begins again. This is a good one to return to again between other activities, as each set of three items makes an entirely new activity.

In case this activity seems too simple, try weaving a story around the Battle of Trenton, Jefferson Davis, and the Battle-ship *Maine*, and see for yourself whether or not the activity is really as easy as it appears at first glance. Such combinations of items will stun all but the stoutest of heart among the history buffs, but watch the youngsters go!

Three or Out

Here is a rapid-fire game which will prove to be the downfall of all but the quickest thinkers in the group. The beginning player chooses a three-letter word such as "hat." He says the word aloud, points to a player, spells the word h a t, and then counts at a moderate rate from one to ten.

While the spelling and counting are going on, his victim (in this game there is no other word for him!) thinks rapidly and frantically in an effort to come forth with the names of three noted Americans whose names begin with the letters h, a, and t. These names (perhaps Hamilton, Arnold, and Tecumseh) he says aloud. If the counter reaches ten before the three people are named, the player naming names takes the place of the counter and remains "it" until he catches a slower thinking victim and is able to pass the chore on. If, however, the person pointed at names three people before the counting concludes, the person who is "it" keeps that distinction and goes hunting for a less alert player.

Decide before playing the game whether or not to allow first names. Most groups will also want to play with a no-repeat rule.

Thus the same three-letter word can't be used twice, but neither can a person's name be used twice.

You will also enjoy this battle of wits using geographical features and points of interest as well as people from history. Don't forget the possibilities offered with writers and others who have a part in the life of America.

Travel by Alphabet

This little play on words can be lots of fun and isn't entirely without value as a learning experience. Players in rotation give the name of a city, state, or the like, and tell in three words why they would like to go there. All three words explaining the reason for going begin with the same letter as does the name of the place the player wishes to visit. The players travel through the alphabet in this fashion, though most groups will do well to omit the letters X and Z if they are confining their travels to the United States. A player who is unable to contribute drops out of play. Players may wish to compile lists of such travel statements as a contest, with the winner being the first to cover the alphabet or perhaps the player with the longest list.

Here are a couple of starters:

"I'd like to go to Alabama to admire agricultural ability."

"I'd like to go to Boston to bake brown beans."

It adds to the flavor of the game if the descriptive words have to do with the place in question. Some players make this a rule of play. Such a rule makes for a bit tougher game but at the same time adds to everyone's fund of knowledge.

We Are Related

Did you ever think that the Statue of Liberty and the city of New York are related? They are, if only for the purpose of this game.

The beginning player gives the others the name of a geographic feature, a structure, a cultural fact, or other identifying feature of a city or town. The first player to name the city or town related to the clue becomes the new leader and receives a point for his thoughtfulness. Sounds easy and it is—for those who know their cities. If the person naming the clue stumps the others, he must give a second clue. Should the group remain in the dark after hearing the second clue, they are enlightened and the leader gets a point for his cleverness. The person to his right then becomes leader, and the game continues.

This little contest gives the traveler a chance to show off his knowledge and allows the would-be traveler to have a chance to dream about what he will see one day.

What's the Name?

This alphabetical listing game is often just the thing for a group of players possessing a reasonable amount of knowledge concerning their nation. The game's object is for each player to complete a list of proper names using every letter of the alphabet as a beginning letter. The number of categories from America should prove to be boundless. A few suggested categories might include military heroes, writers, inventors, religious leaders, politicians, rivers, cities, and so forth.

Decide beforehand whether to use first names to fill the alphabetical list or to limit the listing to last names only. Score on the basis of the first person to complete the list or the greatest number of correct responses at the end of a given time. Try this one, and then come back to it again with different categories, and you will discover it has become a new game.

Where Am I?

An excellent geographical game is "Where Am I?" A player chooses a geographical location and says to the other players,

45

"Where am I?" These players then begin asking questions to discover the place the leader has in mind. The questions they ask must be questions which can be answered either yes or no. Since the world is such a big place, it may be wise to limit chosen locations to the United States, but this does not have to be the case, as shrewd questions will quickly limit the area in question as to continent, state, section of the state, and so on. Good questions concerning industry, agriculture, land forms, population, and other similar items then follow until the location the leader has in mind becomes obvious to at least one guesser.

It works well to have the players ask questions in rotation so that everyone gets a chance to take an active part in the game. When a player thinks he can name the place in question, he may ask if his answer is correct instead of asking a question intended to aid in locating the place. The person who finally locates the place the leader has in mind receives a point and becomes the leader for the next game. If no one has guessed the place after twenty-five questions, the leader gets a point, and the player to his right becomes a new leader.

Stay away from little known towns and villages in this game. The better known places will prove enough of a challenge for most. When the group gets this game well in hand, it may be a good idea to limit the questions to twenty or even to fifteen to make the game better.

As a final note, don't forget that you may use lakes, rivers, mountains, and even man-made structures in this game.

Where Am I From?

Here is a contest of clues and questions which will bring to light a tremendous number of facts from history, geography, and other areas of the social sciences.

The player beginning the game decides on the place from

which he "comes"; this may be a city, state, or even place within a state or city. The first questioner asks him, "Where do you come from?" He replies, "I will not tell you where I come from, but where I come from . . . ," and then tells something about the place he has chosen which will aid in identifying the place. This exchange of questions and answers goes on until a member of the group can correctly identify the place the leader has in mind. The winning player becomes the next leader, and the game begins anew.

The right to question may rotate around the group or may be a group project with one player acting as spokesman. Whenever a person or the group wishes to guess the location the leader has chosen, it may be done after a clue has been given. Only one guess may be offered after any one clue, however. The group should decide whether each member gets a guess in his turn or whether anyone who wishes may guess after a clue is given.

When you present the group with clues, it is always good to begin with rather vague clues and progress to more specific and obvious clues as the game continues. The questions and answers should not be rapid fire but should be given slowly enough so that everyone can consider the clues and attempt to connect them with a given place.

Here is an example as a starter:

"Where do you come from?"

"I will not tell you where I am from, but I live in a major city of America."

"Where do you come from?"

"Where I live there are many office buildings."

"Are you from New York?"

"No, but I am from an Eastern city."

"Are you from Boston?"

"No, but where I do live there are famous statues and monuments."

The questions and answers continue in this manner until the city of Washington, D.C. is guessed and a new leader takes over.

Few games offer the possibilities for giving factual information concerning landmarks, culture, occupations, and so on that this game provides.

After this game has been played and enjoyed, you will certainly enjoy taking a similar tour with us which begins on page 175.

Quizzes
from
History

Discovering the New World

One of the fascinating pages in the nation's history has to do with the men who were responsible for the discovery and exploration of the various parts of the New World. These individuals braved the unknown, hunger, disease, dangers of the wilderness, Indians, and the multitude of other dangers encountered by those entering a new land. For the most part these daring men were driven on by the desire for wealth, though there were a few exceptions. Their treatment of the Indians was usually far from humane. Discounting their greed and often cruel behavior, these men will stand forever in our history as those who dared to open a new world for settlement.

Follow the directions in the following clues, and you should have little difficulty in filling in the title which is now eleven empty spaces. Should you need aid, page 201 will be glad to assist your efforts.

$\overline{1}$ $\overline{2}$ $\overline{3}$ $\overline{4}$ $\overline{5}$ $\overline{6}$ $\overline{7}$ $\overline{8}$ $\overline{9}$ $\overline{10}$ $\overline{11}$

1. If La Salle claimed the land drained by the Mississippi River for France, place the first letter of his name in space four. If he claimed this land for Spain, write the last letter of his name in the fourth space.

2. If Leif Ericson led an expedition to North America nearly five hundred years before Columbus landed, place the first letter of Leif's last name in the first space. If he did not, write the last letter of his name instead.

3. Place in space five an O if Coronado explored the American Southwest, an E if he explored the Southeast.

4. In space eleven place an N if Henry Hudson's name is associated with the *Half Moon* but a W if he sailed in the *Speedwell*.

5. Write a D in space eight if Jacques Marquette was a trader, a T if he was a missionary.

6. If Ponce de Leon searched for the Fountain of Youth, place an X in the second space. If he found the Fountain, change the X to a Z.

7. If the Grand Banks were discovered by Cabot, place an R in space six. If not, place a K there instead.

8. If De Soto had no Indian trouble during his exploration, place an I in space three. If he did have Indian troubles, place a P there instead.

9. If Quebec was founded by Samuel de Champlain, place an O in the tenth space. If he founded New Amsterdam, place a D in the tenth space.

10. If Jacques Cartier explored the St. Lawrence River, place an I in space nine. If he explored the Missouri, place an M in the ninth space.

11. If Henry Hudson was searching for the Northwest Passage, place an A in space seven. If he was hunting for a river into the continent's interior, place an R there instead.

Exploration Criss-Cross

Among the most colorful characters from the American past are those who explored the continent. These men were rugged individuals who overcame great odds in their search for gold, the Northwest Passage, the Indies, and the other quests which led

Europeans to the American shores. All who read about these adventurers find them fascinating, but many are soon confused amid the names which sound foreign to the ear. Perhaps this puzzle will help recall some of these historic names as well as give a point of identification for each of these men.

May we suggest that you use squared paper to build your puzzle or that you clip a sheet of thin paper onto the book page so that you do not write in the book. Answers appear on page 201.

Across

1. This man was the son of Eric the Red.

4. This man claimed the California area for the Spanish.

5. This Frenchman discovered the St. Lawrence.

7. One of the three ships Columbus brought to America

9. This Englishman attempted a colony on Newfoundland.

12. Columbus' ship that was wrecked in the New World

15. A famous attempt at colonization by the English, this colony disappeared without a trace.

16. The old name for Santo Domingo

18. One of the treasures to be found in the Indies

Down

2. Every schoolboy knows this man "sailed the ocean blue in 1492."

3. These men brought Christianity to the New World.

4. A lake bears this Frenchman's name.

6. This Spanish queen is said to have sold her jewels to help Columbus.

8. Another of the ships Columbus brought to America

10. The name of the first white child born in the New World

11. This settler is famous for being saved by an Indian princess.

13. A paper telling where you are and how far you have come

14. Employed by the French, this man explored Narragansett Bay.

(Across cont.)

19. This Spaniard explored the southern U.S. and spread the notion of the Seven Cities of Gold.

(Down cont.)

17. This man gave his name to America.

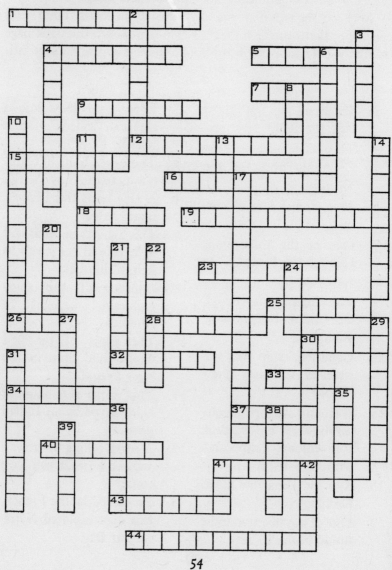

(Across cont.)

23. This man is given the credit for going around the world first, even though he was killed in the Philippines.
25. Columbus gave the natives of the New World this name.
26. This was the direction Columbus wanted to reach, even though he sailed west.
28. Spanish explorer who explored the Tampa Bay area
30. English leader of the famous "Sea Dogs"
32. This man and his son were cast adrift in a bay in the New World and never heard from again.
33. Sailors often caught these and ate them.
34. Many explorers explored these when hunting for the Northwest Passage.
37. The English got their claim to North America from this man's travels.
40. This French explorer attempted to find the mouth of the Mississippi River, failed, and was murdered by his men.

(Down cont.)

20. Rivers were often full of these obstructions which slowed the explorers down.
21. English colonizer who started the "Lost Colony"
22. Spanish explorer who traveled into the interior of the U.S. hunting for the Seven Cities of Gold
24. The division between Spain and Portugal that divided the world was called the _____ of Demarcation.
27. Explorers were after new _____ routes to the East Indies.
29. Englishman sponsored by the East India Co. explored northern U.S. until a crew mutiny forced him to return to England
30. One time governor of Cuba, this man explored the area around the Mississippi and died there.
31. A Jesuit missionary who explored the upper Mississippi River
35. French city in Canada that started as a fur-trading post
36. The trapping partner of thirty-one down

(Across cont.)

41. An exploring Englishman who gave his name to a bay in North America and discovered Greenland

43. The occupation of thirty-six down

44. Conqueror of Puerto Rico and explorer of the coast of Florida

(Down cont.)

38. This man is given credit as the first white man to see the Pacific.

39. Indian boat

41. Sought by trappers

42. Country that paid for Columbus to discover the New World

Land Ho!

Have you ever had the desire to go exploring unknown lands and cross uncharted seas? Almost everyone does have this urge at sometime in his life, but it is impossible for most of us. But we can do the next best thing. We can learn about those men who did explore the world.

Here you have a quiz on explorers. We have supplied the explorer's name. You must give his nationality and what he was noted for. You receive one point for each correct answer, and you lose one point for each incorrect answer. After each man's name you will find a bonus question. If you get the bonus question correct, you get one bonus point. You don't lose any points if you are unable to answer the bonus.

If you need to check your answers, look at page 202. You will also find more information about the explorers with the answers.

If your score is ten or over, you are doing quite well; if it is below ten and above zero, you could do with more knowledge of explorers; and if you drop below zero, you had better spend some time with your history book. If you go right to the top and get twenty or more, you can start looking around for a ship of your own. Bon voyage!

1. Christopher Columbus
   nationality?
   noted for?
   bonus question: Name Columbus' ships—award one point for each correct ship.

2. John Cabot
   nationality?
   noted for?
   bonus questions: 1. For what country did Cabot sail?
      2. Who attempted to steal the credit for his discoveries?

3. Alonso de Ojeda
   nationality?
   noted for?
   bonus question: This man was captain on one of an earlier explorer's ships. Who was the earlier explorer?

4. Pedro Alvares Cabral
   nationality?
   noted for?
   bonus question: Where was Cabral headed when he made his discovery?

5. Sir Francis Drake
   nationality?
   noted for?
   bonus questions: 1. What was the name of his famous flag ship?
      2. What major naval power did he help defeat while in his home country?

6. Leif Ericson
   nationality?
   noted for?
   bonus question: What great island did he discover and name?

7. Bartholomew Gosnold
   nationality?
   noted for?
   bonus question: He aided in establishing the first permanent English colony in the New World. What was it?

8. Henry Hudson
   nationality?
   noted for?
   bonus questions: 1. What was the cruel fate of Hudson?
   2. For what two countries did he sail?
   3. What two things bear his name in the New World today?

9. Ferdinand Magellan
   nationality?
   noted for?
   bonus question: What rewards did Magellan receive for his voyage?

10. Vasco Nunez de Balboa
    nationality?
    noted for?
    bonus question: What was Balboa's position when he sailed from Hispaniola for Ojeda's colony in Columbia?

11. Jean Baptiste Le Moyne Bienville
    nationality?
    noted for?
    bonus question: What great American city did he establish?

12. Cabeza de Vaca
    nationality?
    noted for?
    bonus question: He was the first white man to see an American animal native to the Great Plains. What was this animal?

13. Samuel de Champlain
    nationality?
    noted for?
    bonus questions: 1. What great Canadian city was founded by Champlain?

2. Between which two states is the body of water which bears his name?

14. Francisco Coronado
nationality?
noted for?
bonus question: What great myth initiated his travels?

15. Hernando Cortez
nationality?
noted for?
bonus question: What beast of burden did he introduce to America?

16. Fernando de Soto
nationality?
noted for?
bonus question: What is ironic about his discovery?

17. Louis Joliet
nationality?
noted for?
bonus questions: 1. Who was the Roman Catholic missionary who traveled with Joliet?
2. What was Joliet's occupation?

18. Sieur de La Salle
nationality?
noted for?
bonus question: What great natural wonder was discovered by La Salle?

19. Juan Ponce de Leon
nationality?
noted for?
bonus question: What was this man searching for?

20. Amerigo Vespucci
nationality?
noted for?
bonus question: How did he happen to gain fame?

59

The War of the Revolution

A revolutionary war is never pleasant. Ours was no exception. Many who lived in the colonies had no desire to break away from the mother country of England. Others fiercely desired freedom from English domination. Still others did not care. It is interesting to note that many fled the colonies for the relative safety of Canada in order to avoid the Revolution. Many refused to fight the British, and many who did served for only a few weeks or months before returning to their homes weary of the whole business.

If you correctly answer the ten quiz questions which follow, you should be able to unscramble the ten letters which will appear as a title to the quiz and make from them the word which will correctly title the quiz.

Page 204 provides help should you need it.

$$\overline{1} \quad \overline{2} \quad \overline{3} \quad \overline{4} \quad \overline{5} \quad \overline{6} \quad \overline{7} \quad \overline{8} \quad \overline{9} \quad \overline{10}$$

1. If the Declaration of Independence was written by John Hancock, place an R in the first space. If he did not write that document, place an I there.

2. If General John Burgoyne led German troops in the Revolutionary War, write an O in the second space. If his troops were mostly Scotch, write an E there instead.

3. In the third space write a V if Washington won the Battle of Long Island, a T if he lost.

4. Put a V in the fourth space if the Battle of Bunker Hill was fought on Breed's Hill, an O if it was not.

5. Place an L in the fifth space if the Colonists and Redcoats first met at Concord, a U if they had already met at Lexington.

6. If Benedict Arnold was once a popular Colonial general, place an E in the sixth space; otherwise, write a U in this space.

7. If the Colonial troops fought the British at Valley Forge, place a T in the seventh space; if not, write an L instead.

8. Write an R in space eight if Francis Marion was "the Swamp Fox," an I if he wasn't.

9. If Colonial forces won both the Battle of Trenton and the Battle of Saratoga, place an N in the ninth space. If the English won either or both battles, place an O there instead.

10. If the Tories were Loyalists, write an O in the final space. If the signers of the Declaration were Royalists, place an N in that space.

Men of the Revolution

Men are considered to be great or heroic for a variety of reasons. Some, oddly enough, are for a time considered to be national heroes and at a later date fall from favor for word or deed and are forever looked upon with scorn. From the short clues provided, identify the following men as to last name. When the names are properly identified, those letters indicated by the X below them will spell a word which describes these men for at least a portion of their lives. Page 204 will clear up any rough spots in the quiz.

1. __ __ __ __   This schoolteacher achieved lasting fame
     X   when hanged by the British as a spy.

2. __ __ __ __ __   This man's desire for liberty is often
        X   quoted, but few realize that he was a
                         slaveholder.

3. __ __ __ __ __ __ __ __   This enemy general was
           X   known as "Gentleman
                              Johnny" and was respected
                              by both sides.

4. __ __ __ __ __ __   A daring officer who more than
           X   once saved the day for the Colo-
                         nists, this man is remembered as
                         a traitor.

5. __ __ __ __ __ __ __ __ __   As much as any man,
              X   he proved the pen to
                                 be mightier than the
                                 sword.

6. _ _ _ _ _ _   His financial genius enabled the
      X   Revolution to succeed.

Revolutionary Quickie

Here are a few quick quiz questions designed to give you a hard time. If your responses are correct, the first letters from each answer (those marked with an X) will spell the last name of the first Secretary of the Treasury.

Our choice of answers appears on page 204.

1. _ _ _ _   British general whose brother was a British
  X   admiral in the Revolutionary War

2. _ _ _ _ _ _ _   Associated with a spy named
  X   André to the detriment of both

3. _ _ _ _ _ _ _ _   He might be called the
  X   "Father of the Constitution."

4. _ _ _ _ _ _ _ _ _ _ _   Nickname given
  X   to acts used to punish the people of Boston for the Boston Tea Party

5. _ _ _ _ _ _ _ _ _   Shot heard round the
  X   world

6. _ _ _ _   A person remaining loyal to the British
  X

7. _ _ _ _   The lawyer who organized the committees
  X   of correspondence

8. _ _ _ _ _ _ _ _ _ _   Acts put upon the
  X   Colonists by the British in an attempt to control the commerce of the American colonies

America's Lasting Constitution

At this writing the Constitution has been changed only twenty-four times in almost two hundred years of existence. Ten of those changes were made in the Bill of Rights, or the first ten amendments to the Constitution, which followed close on the heels of the Constitution. The fact that this Constitution, the supreme law of the land, could survive for the length of time it has with so few changes says much for the wisdom of those responsible for its being. Though it often requires the Supreme Court in all its wisdom and experience to interpret the meaning of the Constitution, we are challenging you to test your knowledge of this great document against the quiz which follows. Since the Constitution is the law which is responsible for the total government and legal structure of the nation, all Americans should have more than a passing interest in and awareness of its contents. Score less than thirty correct, and perhaps you should pick up a copy of this historic document and study it briefly, for it is extremely interesting as the quiz may prove. A score of thirty-five or above is excellent, and a perfect score suggests that you either teach American government or have recently read the Constitution word for word.

Good luck on this one. The first twenty questions are multiple choice with only one answer of those given being correct. The second group of twenty statements may be answered either true or false. Correct answers are found on page 204.

Multiple Choice

1. Article I of the Constitution deals with:
    a. Reasons for needing a constitution.
    b. The legislative branch of the federal government.
    c. The freedoms of the citizens of the United States.
    d. The executive branch of the federal government.

2. To be elected to the Senate of the United States, the following qualifications are needed:
    a. Thirty years of age, nine years a citizen of the United States, and live in the state he is going to represent.

    b.   Twenty-five years of age, seven years a citizen, and live in the state he is going to represent.

    c.   Thirty-five years of age, fourteen years in the state he is to represent, and be a natural-born citizen of the United States.

    d.   Five years a resident of the state he is to represent, in the legal profession, and have been in his political party for at least five years.

3. The term "elastic clause" refers to:

    a.   Powers between state and federal governments which stretch one way or the other according to need.

    b.   The secure rights of the United States citizen.

    c.   The enforcement powers of the executive.

    d.   The power given to Congress to pass anything that is "necessary and proper" to enforce the congressional powers.

4. The power to convict a person of impeachment is in the hands of:

    a.   The Supreme Court.

    b.   The Senate.

    c.   The House of Representatives.

    d.   A court made up of voters just for this hearing.

5. The supreme law of the land refers to:

    a.   The Constitution and treaties.

    b.   The Constitution.

    c.   The Constitution, treaties, and laws passed by Congress.

    d.   Treaties and laws passed by Congress.

6. The Constitution:

    a.   Created only the Supreme Court.

    b.   Created the entire federal court system.

    c.   Gave the President of the United States the power to appoint the federal court system.

    d.   Gave the first Supreme Court the duty of creating the lower court system.

7. The term of office for a member of the House of Representatives is:
    a. Two years.
    b. Four years.
    c. Six years.
    d. Eight years.

8. The President of the United States has the power to pardon all of the following except:
    a. A person convicted of high treason.
    b. A murderer.
    c. A person impeached.
    d. A deserter from the armed forces in time of war.

9. According to the Constitution to be tried for treason:
    a. Two witnesses need to testify against you.
    b. The Supreme Court tries the case.
    c. The person needs to have committed this act during wartime.
    d. The President or Vice-President must attend.

10. One of the two amendments forbidden in the Constitution is:
    a. An amendment for the moving of Washington, D.C.
    b. An amendment calling for an increase in number of representatives in the House.
    c. An amendment to cut the number of senators for a given state.
    d. An amendment to change the duties of the presidency.

11. Debts contracted before the Constitution were:
    a. Outlawed because the government under the Constitution had no money.
    b. Considered the responsibility of the individual states.
    c. Nonexistent from the Revolution because the Articles of Confederation had already paid them.
    d. Considered valid, and the new government had to pay.

12. The president of the Constitutional Convention was:

    a. The president under the Articles of Confederation.

    b. Ben Franklin.

    c. George Washington.

    d. John Hancock.

13. The first ___ amendments to the Constitution are called the Bill of Rights.

    a. Eight.

    b. Ten.

    c. Twelve.

    d. Twenty-four.

14. All of the following are rights of accused persons as listed in the Fifth Amendment except:

    a. A person cannot be tried twice for the same crime.

    b. A person cannot be required to testify against himself.

    c. Congress cannot take private property for public use without paying for it.

    d. If a jury is prejudiced, the case may go to another county to be heard.

15. The number of amendments to the Constitution is:

    a. Ten.

    b. Twenty.

    c. Twenty-four.

    d. Thirty.

16. The one amendment to be repealed in United States history was the:

    a. Tenth.

    b. Seventeenth.

    c. Eighteenth.

    d. Twenty-first.

17. The amendment giving women the right to vote was the:

    a. Tenth.

    b. Eighteenth.

    c. Nineteenth.

    d. Twenty-second.

18. The "Lame-duck" amendment refers to:

a. The President is able to be elected only two times or for eight years.
b. The presidential line of succession.
c. Changing the inauguration date from March 4, to January 20.
d. Giving Congress the power to lay and collect income taxes.

19. Citizens of the District of Columbia were given the right to vote for presidential electors in amendment number:
a. Eighteen.
b. Twenty-two.
c. Twenty-three.
d. Thirty.

20. The most widely used method for proposing amendments to the Constitution has been:
a. Two-thirds vote of Congress with ratification by three-fourths of the state legislatures.
b. Two-thirds of the state legislatures requesting Congress to call a constitutional convention.
c. Two-thirds vote of Congress and a majority of voters agreeing in the next election.
d. Majority vote in Congress and have the President sign.

True—False

1. The words "slavery" and "Negro" do not appear in the body of the Constitution.
2. The only qualification for membership in the Supreme Court is to be appointed by the President of the United States and have that appointment agreed upon by the Senate.
3. The only duty for the Vice-President of the United States as mentioned in the Constitution is to preside over the Senate.
4. The importation of slaves was not mentioned in the Constitution.
5. A congressman may not be held for anything he says against another person while he is in Congress.

6. If a congressman commits a murder, he may be tried before the Supreme Court.

7. The House and the Senate may vote raises in salary for themselves.

8. No elected governmental official may stand trial for a murder he has committed until he has been removed from office.

9. The House of Representatives has the power to adjourn for three days without the consent of the Senate.

10. The number of representatives in the House is 435.

11. The President must get senatorial approval for all executive agreements because they are as binding as treaties.

12. Treason is the only crime defined in the Constitution.

13. The President recently granted a title to one of the United States ambassadors to a foreign country so that the ambassador could meet the host country's diplomat on equal terms.

14. Slavery is strictly defined in the Constitution.

15. The Constitution states that the governor of a state must return an escaped prisoner at the request of the other governor.

16. Freedom of religion does not allow a conscientious objector to be forced to bear arms in time of war.

17. The Constitution definitely states how a territory may become a state.

18. The Constitution lists the powers the state governments may exercise as well as the powers the local governments may exercise.

19. The presidential cabinet is definitely provided for in the Constitution by name and number of positions possible.

20. The presidential succession line as established in 1947 is Vice-President, President Pro-Tempore of the Senate, Chief Justice of the Supreme Court, and Speaker of the House.

The War of 1812

The War of 1812 was America's second war with Great Britain. It was not nearly as costly as the Revolution, but neither was a great deal gained by the war. In a sense it was a case of a little nation flexing its growing muscles. Though the war was complete with British invasion of the country, there were few battles and events of great interest in the war. The following questions hit the high points of the war rather quickly. If your answers are correct, the twelve blanks at the head of the quiz will contain the letters spelling the name of one of the great warships of the War of 1812.

Our answers appear on page 205.

$$\overline{1} \ \overline{2} \ \overline{3} \ \overline{4} \ \overline{5} \ \overline{6} \ \overline{7} \ \overline{8} \ \overline{9} \ \overline{10} \ \overline{11} \ \overline{12}$$

1. If impressment of American sailors by England contributed to the War of 1812, place an I in the sixth space; but if this was not a factor, place an I in the seventh space.
2. If Henry Clay, John C. Calhoun, Felix Grundy, and Peter Porter were among those known as War Hawks, write a T in the ninth space. If not all these men favored action against England, write a T in the fourth space.
3. Place an N above number twelve if the battle at Tippecanoe Creek was fought before the War of 1812. If it came after this war, place an N in the second space.
4. If James Monroe was President during the War of 1812, place a U above number five. If James Madison was President at this time, write a U in space eight.
5. If the Americans successfully invaded Canada in 1812, write a C in the first space. If they were not successful in their 1812 invasion attempts, place a C above number nine.
6. If Oliver Hazard Perry was a noteworthy general during the War of 1812, place an O in space eight. If his fame was earned as a naval officer, place an O in the eleventh space.
7. If the British invaded Pittsburgh during the War of 1812, place an S in the second space. If instead they invaded Washington, D.C., place an S in the fourth space.
8. If "America" was written as the result of a bombardment during the War of 1812, write a T in space ten. If "The Star-

Spangled Banner" was written for that reason, place a T̲ in the seventh space.

9. If Jean Laffite and his pirates sided with the Americans against the British at the Battle of New Orleans, place an O̲ in the second space. If he aided the British, place an O̲ in the first box.

10. If the Battle of New Orleans occurred during the War of 1812, write an I̲ in space nine. If it came after the war was over, place an I̲ in space ten.

11. If "Stonewall" Jackson fought the British during the War of 1812, write an N̲ in the fourth space. If "Old Hickory" Jackson fought at New Orleans, write an N̲ in the third space.

12. If "Old Ironsides" was the *United States*, place a T̲ in the sixth space. If she was the *Constitution*, place a T̲ in fifth space.

North and South in Conflict

Never in the history of the American nation has there been a war with such tragic results as those of the Civil War. The scars of this war still exist in the heart and mind of the nation today.

Follow the instructions given in the quiz below to spell a word which came to be known and accepted as a name for members of one great army during the Civil War. Though you shouldn't encounter any real difficulties, page 205 will help you if you need aid.

$$\overline{1} \quad \overline{2} \quad \overline{3} \quad \overline{4} \quad \overline{5} \quad \overline{6} \quad \overline{7} \quad \overline{8} \quad \overline{9} \quad \overline{10} \; \overline{11}$$

1. If the South won the First Battle of Bull Run, place a C̲ in the first space; but if they lost this battle, place a K̲ there instead.

2. If all the following are Confederate generals, place a U̲ in the second space; if not, write an O̲: Hooker, Mead, Jackson, Lee.

3. If South Carolina was the first state to secede from the

Union, place an N in the third space; if not, place an L in that space.

4. If Lee twice invaded the North, write an F in the next space; otherwise, place a V there.

5. Place an O in the next space if Sheridan captured Atlanta; an E if Sherman did.

6. In the sixth space place a D if Jeb Stuart was a Confederate cavalry general; an O if he led infantry.

7. If Lincoln asked Lee to lead Union forces, place an E in the seventh space; if not, write a W instead.

8. Place an R in the next space if Montgomery, Alabama, was the Confederate capital before Richmond, Virginia; an F if it was not.

9. If the Confederate flag contained eleven stars, place a B in the next space. If it contained thirteen stars, write an A instead.

10. If West Virginia was a member of the Confederacy, place an I in the tenth space; otherwise, place a T in that space.

11. In the final space write a Z if Grant surrendered to Lee at Appomattox Court House; an E if Lee surrendered to Grant.

Civil War Quickie

This quiz is designed to fill a spare moment or two of your time. When each clue has led you to a correct answer, the first letters of the answers (we've marked them with an X so they will catch your eye) will spell the last name of a great leader of the Civil War.

Correct answers appear on page 205.

1. __ __ __ __ __ __ __ __ __ __   A Confederate gen-
    X   eral who fought at
                                              Gettysburg

2. __ __ __ __ __ __ __ __   The sixteenth American
    X   President was from this
                                        state.

3. _ _ _ _ _   A section of the nation which in gen-
   X   eral opposed slavery
4. _ _ _ _   Senator from the West who was known as
   X   "the Great Compromiser"
5. _ _ _   Union general who was postwar commander
   X   of the South
6. _ _ _   Commander of the Army of Northern Vir-
   X   ginia
7. _ _ _ _ _ _ _   People the Northern states
   X   sought to free

Civil Cross-Up

Before you begin this little brain tickler, we suggest that you build your puzzle on squared paper or that you paper clip a transparent sheet of paper onto the page and write on it.

Simply follow the clues and make sure each name fits its assigned space and crosses correctly with the other names, and your puzzle will work itself—almost. Besides having fun we guarantee you will know more about personages of the Civil War than you did when you began.

The puzzle's solution may be found on page 205.

Across

2. One of the corps commanders at Gettysburg
5. A famous male hairstyle came from this Union general's name.
7. This Confederate general commanded forces at the First Battle of Bull Run.
8. A Union general at Gettysburg that advanced too far for safe support

Down

1. This man was called "Stonewall."
3. Another corps commander at Gettysburg
4. Headed the Army of the Potomac at the First Battle of Bull Run
6. This famous Union general moved too slowly.
9. The major Confederate cavalry leader

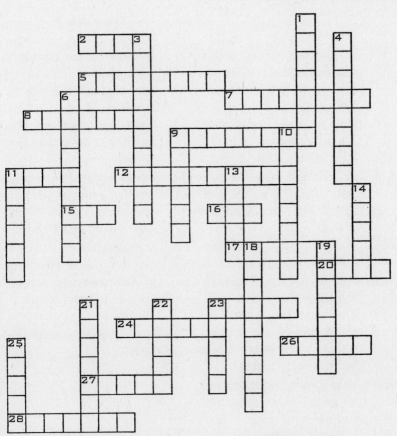

(Across cont.)

9. This Union cavalry leader destroyed the Shenandoah Valley.

11. Commanded the Army of the Potomac at the Second Battle of Bull Run

12. Confederate commander at Charleston harbor

15. Famous commander of the Army of Northern Virginia

(Down cont.)

10. The major in charge of the fort in Charleston harbor

11. Union admiral at Vicksburg and New Orleans

13. Union commander at the end of the war

14. Leader of the Third Corps of the Confederate force at Gettysburg

(Across *cont.*)

16. Nickname for six down

17. Although commanders are important, most of the work was done by these people.

20. This man has been called Lee's "maverick" general.

23. This man's army arrived at Pittsburg Landing and was responsible for the defeat of the Confederates.

24. This man fought in the Civil War but is more famous for his death at the Little Big Horn.

26. This man was placed in command of the Union forces just before the battle of Gettysburg.

27. This Confederate general led a raid on Washington.

28. Commanded the Confederate cavalry after the death of Stuart

(Down *cont.*)

18. Union general at the Battle of Chickamauga

19. This man is famous for his march through a Southern state.

21. Confederate general that led the attack on Fort Pillow

22. Confederate cavalry leader that fought in the Shenandoah Valley and was killed at Harrisonburg, in 1862

23. Commander of the Army of Tennessee and later advisor to Jefferson Davis

25. This man surrendered the last major Confederate forces.

America's Territorial Growth

As new territory was added to the nation, the area grew and expanded. It may grow again in the future if the people of Puerto Rico have their wishes granted. The United States has grown by great amounts when the territory added was large. At other times one could scarcely notice the difference in the size of the country after another territory was added. Some of the land added to the country was purchased, some acquired by treaty when Americans traded for the land gained, and some was taken by force.

Here we have a record of eleven territorial additions to the country during the 1800's. Some of the territory included was not admitted to statehood until the twentieth century, however. We have provided the year in which the territory was officially acquired and the name by which the acquisition was known. You might see whether you can name the states and parts of states carved from the territory. We'll even provide the number of states involved in parentheses following the territorial name.

You will need a score of twenty-five to pass, thirty to be in the average area, thirty-five to be considered far above average, forty to be superior, and forty-two to be perfect.

When you have given this toughie your all, check with page 205 for the results.

1. 1803—Louisiana Purchase (13)
2. 1810—Annexation of 1810 (1)
3. 1813—Annexation of 1813 (2)
4. 1818—British Compromise (3)
5. 1819—Spanish Cession (1)
6. 1845—Annexation of Texas (6)
7. 1846—Oregon Compromise (5)
8. 1848—Mexican Cession (7)
9. 1853—Gadsden Purchase (2)
10. 1867—Alaska Purchase (1)
11. 1898—Annexation of Hawaii (1)

(Those last two shouldn't have given you much trouble.)

Growth of the Union

The United States grew as new territories were purchased or won. States cut from these new areas could, of course, not enter the Union until population reached the point that statehood could be justified. Other items also had a part in determining when an area might become a state.

Using what you know about the order in which the U.S. added new territories to the nation, about geographical influences on population growth, about gold and land rushes, and about any other factors which might cause states to be created, see if you can arrange the twenty states which follow into the order in which they joined the Union.

You will probably enjoy challenging yourself further by giving the year in which each state entered the Union.

This is an excellent quiz for the person who likes to reason things through. In this case, thinking in terms of history should enable you to complete the quiz with few, if any, errors.

Page 206 will let you know how well you reasoned.

Arizona	Vermont
North Carolina	Missouri
Maine	Florida
Hawaii	Alaska
Delaware	Utah
California	West Virginia
Montana	Ohio
Illinois	Rhode Island
Oklahoma	Colorado
Massachusetts	Tennessee

America's First Citizens

There can be little doubt that the most tragic chapter in American history is that dealing with the relations between settlers, explorers, the government, and the American Indian. No one will dispute the fact that the Indians often inflicted terrible injuries upon the advancing members of the nation-to-be. Neither can anyone deny the fact that the Indians were often the victims of cruelty, deceit, and greed.

We have chosen twenty of the famous Indians in American history to play a part in this next quiz. Some were known for the havoc they caused, while others were known as great and willing friends of the advancing tide of Americans. All are famous in their own right.

See if you can match these great names with the brief descriptions which follow. Many will be easy; a few will prove a bit more difficult. Any score above fifteen will be considered as passing, but why not go all the way and have a perfect score?

Turn to page 206 for confirmation of your choices.

Billy Bowlegs	Osceola
Sacajawea	Ouray
Squanto	Sitting Bull
Pontiac	Tecumseh
Powhatan	Geronimo
Weatherford	Chief Joseph
Opechancanough	Wildcat
Pocahontas	King Philip
Cochise	Little Turtle
Black Hawk	Logan

1. Who was the father of Pocahontas?
2. Who married John Rolfe?
3. Which great Indian befriended the Pilgrims?
4. What Indian led his followers against the New England settlers in 1675 and 1676?
5. Who was the Ottawa chief who lead a rebellion against the English in 1763?
6. General George Custer was defeated by this chieftain at the Battle of the Little Big Horn.
7. The Lewis and Clark expedition was aided by the services of this Indian.
8. The activities of this Shawnee chief were in part responsible for the battle at Tippecanoe Creek.
9. Who was the great Ute chief from Colorado?
10. This Apache chief led the last major Indian uprising in the Southwest. He was pursued by United States troops across Arizona and New Mexico before being captured.
11. Which great Apache chief made peace in 1872 with the whites?

12. A famous speech dealing with the miseries and suffering of Indians at the hands of the white men was made by this great Indian leader.

13. Who was the Creek Indian chief who Andrew Jackson defeated in Florida in 1818?

14. Who was the chief of the Florida Seminoles who led the war against the white man in 1836? He was imprisoned when he came under a flag of truce to talk with white military authorities and died in prison.

15. He led the Nez Percé Indians in the tragic war of 1877.

16. This Pamunkey war chief fought against the Virginia settlers from 1622 to 1644. Powhatan was his older brother.

17. The forces of "Mad" Anthony Wayne subdued this Indian who said of the final treaty, "I am the last to sign it and I will be the last to break it."

18. In 1813 this Creek chief led the Fort Mims massacre in which 536 men, women, and children died.

19. A war in which both Abe Lincoln and Jefferson Davis fought on the same side in 1831 was named for this man.

20. A warrior imprisoned with Osceola in Fort Marion escaped and led his forces against Colonel Zachary Taylor at the Okeechobee River. Who was he?

The Wildest of the West

The West is at best a relative term. In 1750, it meant what is now the state of Kentucky. By 1800, Missouri was considered to be the West. Fifty years later, California held claim to being the West. Today, anything west of the Mississippi River is the West to many Americans, and those states comprising the Rocky Mountain Empire are the West to nearly everyone.

There is nothing relative about the wildness of those who were noted for being the "wildest in the West." This is not to say that all these people were desperadoes, for they were not. It is to say, however, that in one way or another they displayed a wildness and/or courage not commonly seen.

We'll give you the names of fifteen individuals whose names will long live in the history and folklore of the American West. Whether you can match them with their identifying items depends upon how well you have paid attention to your American history over the years. A score of less than ten should send you running for cover. It takes twelve correct answers to achieve anything like a really respectable score. From there upwards to a perfect score, we are happy with your efforts.

Our answers appear on page 206.

Here are the "Wildest of the West":

Wild Bill Hickok	William Cody	Bill Tilghman
Jim Bridger	James Bowie	Jesse James
Bat Masterson	Calamity Jane	Kit Carson
Daniel Boone	Pat Garrett	Jedediah Smith
William Quantrill	Wyatt Earp	Bob Dalton

Here is what they did:

1. This was the sheriff who killed Billy the Kid.

2. What Dodge City sheriff eventually became a deputy United States marshal in New York City and held that post until his death in 1921?

3. In the 1880's, this man was a United States marshal in Tombstone. With his two town marshal brothers and Doc Holliday, he took part in the O.K. Corral shooting in 1881.

4. Chased from Kansas by a detachment of General Sheridan's cavalry in 1870 this man later returned as marshal of Abilene, Kansas.

5. For fifty years this quiet lawman kept the peace in Dodge City, Kansas, and other cities in Oklahoma, until at the age of seventy-five he was killed in Cromwell, Oklahoma, by a drunken prohibition officer.

6. A friend of such men as Tom Fitzpatrick and Jed Smith, this mountain man was famous as a storyteller. His tales even included stories from Shakespeare's plays. Each year a Boy Scout troop visits his grave and places a wreath at the base of the monument.

7. In the 1770's, this man crossed the Cumberlands into Kentucky. His route later became the great Wilderness Road.

8. A noted frontiersman, this redheaded man married the goddaughter of the Mexican general Santa Anna whose forces later killed the gallant American at the Battle of the Alamo.

9. Christened Christopher, this hunter and trapper achieved fame as an army scout in the 1840's when he led General Frémont into the Rocky Mountains.

10. One of the more religious of the early trappers and traders, this man was noted for his fairness. He died at the age of thirty-two while guiding a caravan to Santa Fé.

11. Known as a buffalo hunter and plainsman, this man organized a wild west show which carried the adventure of the early West to the world.

12. One of the most famous frontier characters, this woman was known for her horsemanship, marksmanship, and hard-drinking. Disgused as a man, she accompanied several expeditions into wild territory in the mid 1870's.

13. This daring member of Quantrill's Raiders during the Civil War later led an outlaw band on a series of bank and train robberies through the midwest. In 1882, a member of his band, Robert Ford, killed him for an offered reward.

14. In 1892, this former United States Indian marshal met his end when he and his gang attempted to rob the Coffeyville, Kansas, bank.

15. This former schoolteacher organized a band of Confederate irregular cavalry and led them on a series of criminal and near-criminal raids, notable among which was the pillage and slaughter at Lawrence, Kansas, in 1863. He died in 1865, in a federal prison.

Beginnings

Much of what is called "modern America" found its beginning in the troubled and turbulent years after the Civil War. We have collected some of those "beginnings" and put them in a short quiz. If you have difficulty with any of the answers, turn to page 207.

If you are interested in scoring the quiz, give yourself one point for each correct answer and subtract three points for each incorrect answer. If you end up with a plus score, tell Perry Mason to move over and make room for a new detective.

1. What organization, designed to maintain white supremacy in the South, was formed on December 24, 1865, in the law office of Thomas M. Jones in Pulaski, Tennessee?

2. On May 16, 1865, a five-cent coin was issued, and we still use it. What is it called?

3. A society designed to prevent cruelty to animals was formed on April 10, 1865. It is still in existence today. What is it?

4. Although originally outsold by pipes and cigars, this tobacco product appeared in American markets for the first time in 1867. What is it?

5. On September 1, 1869, this political party was organized. The final triumph of the party was the Eighteenth Amendment. What party are we thinking of?

6. In 1872, America's first mail-order house was organized in Chicago, Illinois. Their first catalogue was a single sheet of paper. Now it is best measured in pounds. What mail-order house do we have in mind?

7. *Harper's Weekly* published a cartoon by Thomas Nast in 1870. The cartoon used for the first time a donkey to symbolize a political party. What party was symbolized?

8. On June 10, 1878, a woman's suffrage amendment was introduced by Senator A. A. Sargent. What amendment was this, and when was it finally passed? (Score each part of the question separately.)

9. On January 28, 1878, the first telephone exchange opened in what American city?

10. 1879 saw the first successful five-and-ten-cent-store. Who was the famous American businessman who put it together?

11. In 1881, the American Red Cross was organized in Wash-

ington, D.C. It received a federal charter in 1900. Who was the great American woman who organized the Red Cross?

12. "Do you have a problem?" In 1878, Mrs. Elizabeth M. Gilmore began the first "advice to the lovelorn" column. By what name is Mrs. Gilmore usually known?

13. What event took place on January 10, 1901, near Beaumont, Texas, that completely reorganized the economy of Texas?

14. In 1903, Americans saw their first movie with a plot. It is interesting to note that it was a western. What was the title of this motion picture?

15. On July 4, 1903, the first Pacific cable opened, and the President of the U.S. sent a message around the world in twelve minutes. Who was that President?

16. On December 17, 1903, the age of air was ushered in by two brothers at Kitty Hawk, North Carolina. Who were those first airmen? (Both names must be given for one point.)

17. In 1905, the I.W.W. was established in Chicago. What does I.W.W. stand for?

18. On Christmas Eve, 1906, the first known program of voice and music was broadcast. Then in 1920, radio got its real beginning when station KDKA, Pittsburgh, Pennsylvania, broadcast the election returns of the Harding-Cox election. Radio now has four great networks. Can you name them? (Each is considered a separate question.)

19. In 1909, the NAACP was organized. What do the letters stand for?

20. In 1913, the first assembly line was set in motion. Who was the great American industrialist responsible for this?

Headlines

Here are some headlines that might have appeared in the national newspapers in the years between the Civil War and World War I. Unfortunately someone has left out some of the vital information. It is your job to supply the missing fact or facts.

We have included an example so you will be able to see what the culprit has done to all our news clippings.

The _____ War ends, April 9, 1865. Now, what war was that? Civil. Right. See how easy it is? If you happen to get stuck, which we don't anticipate, you will find answers on page 207.

1. President __(name)__ was shot yesterday evening, April 14, 1865, while attending a performance at __(name)__ Theater.

2. The greatest single maritime disaster in the history of the sea occurred yesterday, April 27, when the __(ship)__ exploded on the Mississippi River. She was returning Union prisoners of war to their homes in the North.

3. The _____ Amendment was adopted today, December 18, 1865. This amendment gives the slaves their freedom.

4. Finally after repeated failure and frustration the __(ship)__ completed the laying of the Atlantic Cable, July 27, 1866.

5. The Senate began impeachment proceedings today, March 13, 1868, against __(president)__ for removing Secretary Stanton from the office of _____, thereby breaking the Tenure of Office Act.

6. March 16, 1868, President __(name)__ is found not guilty.

7. Congress sets precedent! June 25, 1868, Congress passed __(length)__ hour day for government employees.

8. The _____ Amendment giving the Negroes United States citizenship was adopted yesterday, July 14, 1869.

9. We just received word that the Transcontinental _____ _____ was completed May 10, 1869, at Promontory Point, __(state)__ .

10. The world of men was shaken at its very base this week when the __(name)__ Territory granted on December 10, 1869, suffrage for women.

11. Today, March 30, 1870, the Fifteenth Amendment to the Constitution was adopted. This amendment granted_____ the right to vote.

12. On June 25, 1876, General George A. Custer and 265 men of the 7th Cavalry were slaughtered at ____(site)____, Montana, by Sioux Indians. The Indians were led by ___(name)___ .

13. Tragedy! The President has been shot! President ___(name)___ was shot in a Washington, D.C., railway station by _____(name)_____ , July 2, 1881.

14. President ____(name)____ unveiled the Statue of Liberty today, October 28, 1886, at a ceremony on ___(name)___ Island, the new home of the statue. Miss Liberty is a gift to the American people from ___(country)___ honoring ___(number)___ years of American independence.

15. May 31, 1889, Johnstown, ___(state)___ , suffered one of the greatest tragedies in American history when a (structure) above the city broke and covered the city with over thirty feet of _____.

16. War was declared today, July 2, 1890, on big business with the passing of the _____ Antitrust Act.

17. The President was highly criticized by the press when his ___(name of new tariff)___ became law today, October 1, 1890. This is the ___(highest—lowest)___ tariff in this country's history.

18. Congress created today, March 3, 1891, the ___(new judicial addition)___ to take some of the load off the Supreme Court.

19. The Supreme Court, May 18, 1896, gave its verdict on the now famous _____ v. Ferguson case. The Court supported the "separate but _____" idea of segregation.

20. We received word that on August 12, 1896, gold was discovered in the _____ region of Alaska. The discovery was made about three miles from the town of _____, just over the Alaskan border in ___(country)___.

21. February 9, 1898, a letter by the ___(country)___ minister, Dupuy de Lôme, was intercepted in Cuba and published by the _____ press. It contained damaging remarks about President ___(president's name)___.

22. February 15, 1898, the ___(ship)___ was blown up in ___(city)___ harbor, Cuba!

23. Word has been received that Spain has officially, on April 24, 1898, recognized that a state of war exists between her and ___(country)___.

24. August 9, 1898, ___(country)___ accepts United States peace terms. The war is over!

25. Paris, December 10, 1898, the peace treaty between ___(country)___ and ___(country)___ was signed today by representatives of the belligerents.

26. September 8, 1900, a hurricane struck ___(city)___ today driving Gulf waters over the land. In this disaster over 6,000 persons perished.

27. March 2, 1901, Congress today adopted the ___(name)___ Amendment which insists that the new Cuban constitution include a series of U.S. provisions before U.S. military forces are withdrawn from Cuba. Needless to say, the amendment is not popular in Cuba.

28. September 6, 1901, President ___(name)___ was shot while attending the ___(event)___ in Buffalo, New York. He was shot by Leon F. Czolgosz.

29. President ___(name)___ died today, September 14, 1901, in Canton, Ohio.

30. Congress, June 28, 1902, passed the Isthmian Canal Act authorizing the financing and building of the ___(canal)___ .

31. November 2, 1903, President ___(name)___ ordered U.S. warships to ___(country)___ to maintain "free and uninterrupted transit" across the isthmus. It is the feeling of most learned gentlemen that the President's real reason is to assure the success of the ___(country)___ independence movement against Columbia.

32. Today, November 3, 1903, the federal government recognized ___(country)___ independence. This is by far the fastest recognition ever accorded any new nation by the United States.

33. July 11, 1905, ___(country)___ and ___(country)___ accepted President Roosevelt's proposal for a "peace parley."

34. Representatives of the belligerent nations at the Presi-

dent's "peace parley" _(did or did not)_ sign a treaty of peace on September 5, 1905, at Portsmouth, New Hampshire.

35. June 30, 1906, _(name of act)_ became law today. The bill provides for accurate labeling and inspection of many consumer goods. Informed sources feel that more legislation of this nature will soon be enacted.

36. President _(name)_ signed the Sixteenth Amendment today, July 12, 1909, legalizing _____ .

37. The Cunard White Star liner, _(ship's name)_ struck an _____ on her maiden voyage and sank early this morning, April 15, 1912.

38. June 18, 1912, ex-president _(name)_ and his followers walked out of the _(party)_ Convention and formed the _(name)_ or Bull Moose Party.

39. May 31, 1913, the Seventeenth Amendment was adopted today making the popular election of _(legislators)_ law.

40. October 10, 1913, the _____ Canal is completed.

The Melting Pot

The United States has become a nation of united nationalities. The U.S. accepted and made welcome the "tired" and "poor" of the world and has benefited as much from their presence as they have in being here. We have collected the names of some famous Americans who either immigrated to this country, or whose family chose the United States. Of course, all Americans can claim ancestors from some foreign land, with the exception of the Indians, but those individuals chosen by us are usually identified with their homeland.

You receive one point for nationality and one point for the individual's achievement. If you miss no more than three, you are doing very well indeed; more than five, and you could do with some study; more than ten, and you should take a look at a good biographical dictionary.

This also makes a good game. One person names an individual, and the others must name his homeland and what he is noted for.

If you need some answers to our questions, turn to page 208.

1. Enrico Fermi   nationality?   noted for?
2. Lou Gehrig   nationality?   noted for?
3. Eddie Cantor   nationality?   noted for?
4. Leopold Stokowski   nationality?   noted for?
5. Spyros Skouras   nationality?   noted for?
6. Daniel Webster   nationality?   noted for?
7. Rocky Marciano   nationality?   noted for?
8. George Balanchine   nationality?   noted for?
9. Priscilla Mullens   nationality?   noted for?
10. Samuel Gompers   nationality?   noted for?
11. Carl Sandburg   nationality?   noted for?
12. Joe DiMaggio   nationality?   noted for?
13. Yma Sumac   nationality?   noted for?
14. Philip Schuyler   nationality?   noted for?
15. Stan Musial   nationality?   noted for?
16. John Paul Jones   nationality?   noted for?
17. Eugene O'Neill   nationality?   noted for?
18. Fiorello La Guardia   nationality?   noted for?
19. Cornelius Vanderbilt   nationality?   noted for?
20. John Ericsson   nationality?   noted for?
21. Dick Haymes   nationality?   noted for?
22. John Van Druten   nationality?   noted for?
23. Gene Krupa   nationality?   noted for?
24. John F. Kennedy   nationality?   noted for?
25. Jonas Salk   nationality?   noted for?
26. Baron von Steuben   nationality?   noted for?
27. Jack Dempsey   nationality?   noted for?
28. Lafayette   nationality?   noted for?
29. Charles Lindbergh   nationality?   noted for?
30. Albert Einstein   nationality?   noted for?

Headliners of the '20's and a Bit Before

Here's a chance to take a close look at some of those wild and exciting days and people of the "Roaring Twenties." We have collected a number of items and listed them in seven groups according to their nature. For instance, we have listed four important sporting events. Now it is your job to put the events in the order in which they occurred. If you get them all right, you can call yourself F. Scott Fitzgerald. If you miss one or two, you still qualify as a member of the "Lost Generation." If you miss three or more, you've not been reading enough Hemingway and keeping up with your "Charleston."

Ready? Got your raccoon coat on?

Sports:

Jack Dempsey defeated by Gene Tunney.

Red Grange played first professional football game with the Chicago Bears.

Dempsey KO'd Jess Willard in the third round at Toledo.

Babe Ruth hit sixty home runs.

Travel:

Navy NC-4 crossed the Atlantic to Azores.

Charles A. Lindbergh, "Lucky Lindy," flew solo across the Atlantic Ocean.

The Model A Ford was shown.

The "Twenties" in high places:

Elk Hills Reserve leased to Edward L. Doheny's Pan American Oil Company.

Warren G. Harding becomes President with the greatest percentage of popular votes in presidential history. (F.D.R. beat his record in the election of 1936.)

Teapot Dome Reserve leased to Harry F. Sinclair and Mammoth Oil Company.

Harding dies in office.

Crime and Court:

Bobby Franks kidnapped and killed by Leopold and Loeb.

Arnold Rothstein died of gunshot wounds.

Seven gangsters killed in the Saint Valentine's Day massacre.

Scopes trial ends. Scopes was convicted.

Attorney General A. Mitchell Palmer leads "communist" raids.

Holdup-killing at Braintree, Massachusetts, which involved two immigrants, Sacco and Vanzetti.

The Hall-Mills murder case.

The House of Morgan bombed. (Sometimes referred to as the Wall Street bombing.)

Documents of the "Jazz Era":
Nineteenth Amendment became law giving women the right to vote in national elections.

Armistice signed. World War I ends.

Thirty-sixth state ratified the Eighteenth or Prohibition Amendment.

"Arms Parley" began meeting.

Boom to Bust:
Calvin Coolidge becomes President.

Black Friday. Stock market crashed, ushering in the Great Depression.

Herbert Hoover inaugurated.

Never Befores:
Boston police strike.

After 18 days trapped in a Kentucky cave, Floyd Collins dies.

KDKA in East Pittsburgh became America's first broadcasting station.

Atlantic City holds first beauty contest.

Emile Coué arrives from France and says to millions, "Day by day in every way I am getting better and better."

Did you get them all? If you want to compare your answers with ours, look at page 209.

World War II Dictionary

Do you know what a mulberry is? Well, work this quiz and you will find out. We have collected thirty war words. Your task is to tell what the word means. If you get them all, it is assumed that you were there. If you miss one or two, you knew someone who was there. If you miss three or four, you have read about someone who was there. And if you miss five or more, you just haven't been there, either in fact or fiction.

1. Fish	11. Mulberry	21. V-J Day
2. Blitzkrieg	12. Gooney bird	22. Car pool
3. Snafu	13. LST	23. V-E Day
4. Sitzkrieg	14. Potato masher	24. Flat top
5. Jeep	15. Fort	25. Ashcans
6. A-bomb	16. Kamikaze	26. Tokyo express
7. G.I.	17. Quisling	27. Wolf pack
8. J.G.	18. The Hump	28. Hedgehog
9. K.P.	19. Island hopping	29. Window
10. Battlewagon	20. Buzz bomb	30. "Mighty Mo"

World War II Nicknames

World War II for all its size and complexity was a very personal war. It touched more lives and had a greater effect on the course of world events than any other conflict in the history of man, and yet the individual leaders came to be known and spoken of as friends and neighbors. Their likes, dislikes, habits, and attitudes were top news items.

One thing that most of World War II's personalities had in common was a nickname. We have gathered some of the most common ones from America and abroad for you to identify. We name the nickname, and you give the person's whole name. If you get them all, you either have been doing some outside reading, or you were there. If you miss one or two, well . . . you are still a medal winner. More than three misses, and you best catch a few of those late movies on TV dealing with the war.

Here we go. An easy one to start.

1. "Monty"	4. "Winnie"
2. "Ike"	5. "Vinegar Joe"
3. "Blood and Guts"	6. "Mac"

7.	"Desert Fox"	14.	"Tokyo Rose"
8.	"Skinny"	15.	"The Good Gray Judge"
9.	"Bull"	16.	"Uncle Joe"
10.	"Il Duce"	17.	"Highly Delightful"
11.	"Hap"	18.	"F.D.R."
12.	"Lord Haw Haw"	19.	"Clemmie"
13.	"Der Fuehrer"	20.	"Pappy"

Page 211 gives the correct answers, but don't give up too easily.

Ships as Makers of History

Without ships the last 350 years of American history would never have been written. Without ships most of the great wars in which the United States has engaged would never have been fought. Without ships the world of today would be much changed. In a sense, the history of ships is the history of the modern world.

Here are twenty-five ships that have played a decided role in the history of the United States, though not always for the good of the country. In one instance this role was an indirect role affecting the history.

With a little study of the history of great ships one might well add several hundred names to our honor roll. We would encourage this, as these ships and their careers teach history in as fascinating a manner as is possible.

Don't be discouraged if you run aground. The consequences won't be nearly so harsh as those seen at the head of the description column. Let's cast off now and bring this quiz around in record time. When you drop anchor at the end of the quiz, turn to page 212 for confirmation of your chosen answers.

Ship name	Description
1. *Pinta*	A. A British customs ship burned when it went aground chasing a Colonial vessel.

2. Half Moon

3. Mayflower

4. Niña

5. Speedwell

6. Liberty

7. Dartmouth

8. Gaspee

9. Maine

10. Flying Cloud

11. Ranger

12. Alabama

13. Constitution

14. Monitor

15. Santa Maria

16. Merrimac

17. Matthew

18. Victoria

19. Columbia

B. Sailed by Henry Hudson

C. Called "Fulton's Folly"

D. A British ship which was captured during the Revolution and returned to the Colonies flying an American flag

E. A victim of "Old Ironsides"

F. On the decks of this ship the Japanese surrendered ending World War II.

G. Ship owned by John Hancock

H. Later known as the Merrimac

I. Sailed by John Paul Jones against the Serapis

J. The first American man-of-war to fly the "Stars and Stripes"

K. Carried the Pilgrims

L. Carried the Pilgrims, but not to America

M. Captain Robert Gray's ship when the Columbia River in Oregon was discovered

N. John Cabot's ship

O. Carried tea to Boston

P. An infamous Confederate raider

Q. Sank the Union ships Congress and Cumberland

R. First ship to sail around the world

S. The sinking of this ship in Havana harbor on February

15, 1898, led to the Spanish
20. *Virginia*   American War.

T. Union ironclad with a revolv-
21. *Bonhomme Richard*   ing turret and often called
"cheesebox on a raft"

22. *Serapis*   U. Fast clipper ship sailing from
New York to San Francisco

23. *Clermont*   V. Oldest ship in the United
States Navy, built in the
24. *Guerrière*   1790's, served in the War of
1812 where it became known
25. *Missouri*   as "Old Ironsides"

W. Ship sailing with Columbus
(use for three ships)

America, a Land of Connections

America's history is one of expanding lines of transporation and communication. Some extremely important links of yesterday are all but forgotten today. Others are in daily use many years after being built. Here are twenty important connecting links in history. Some are very old, some not so old. All were important; some are still of great importance.

Matching all of the connecting links with the points they connected qualifies you as a true student of history. One or two errors give you an above average score. Up to five mistakes is still a good score, but you can't miss more than eight and pass.

Page 212 will answer any questions after you finish.

Here are the names by which these great links were commonly known:

Welland Ship Canal   Potomac Canal (America's first)
Oregon Trail (use twice)   Erie Canal
Santa Fé Trail   George Washington Bridge
Cumberland Road   Transatlantic Cable
St. Lawrence Seaway   Alcan Highway
Pony Express   New York Central Company

Braddock's Road   Missouri Pacific Railroad
Mormon Trail   Illinois and Michigan Canal
Old National Road   Pennsylvania Portage and Canal
Panama Canal   System

And here are the points connected:

1. St. Joseph, Missouri, and San Francisco, California
2. Albany and Buffalo, New York
3. The Atlantic and Pacific Oceans
4. Fort Cumberland and Fort Pitt
5. Cumberland, Maryland, and Wheeling, West Virginia
6. Lakes Erie and Ontario
7. Lake Michigan and the Illinois River
8. Independence, Missouri, and Astoria, Washington
9. St. Louis and Kansas City, Missouri
10. New York and Buffalo, New York
11. Kansas City, Missouri, and Santa Fé, New Mexico
12. Omaha, Nebraska, and Salt Lake City, Utah
13. Dawson Creek, British Columbia, and Fairbanks, Alaska
14. Omaha, Nebraska, and Portland, Oregon
15. The United States and Great Britain
16. Philadelphia and Pittsburgh, Pennsylvania
17. Cumberland, Maryland, and the Ohio River at Wheeling
18. Washington, D.C., and Cumberland, Maryland
19. New York and New Jersey
20. The Great Lakes and the Atlantic Ocean

North, South, East, and West

Have you ever stopped to think what an important part compass directions play in our lives? Here is a little quiz which makes use of the points of the compass in reviewing some interesting points in American history.

If you can correctly fill the blanks in all twenty statements, you have a good command of the facts which make up the nation's history and probably could get an "A" in any history course. One or two errors, and you are probably a "B" student in history. A "C" student will have from three to six errors. Take time to think, and you will pass with flying colors.

Take a look at page 212 for the answers.

Oh yes, don't forget that words such as northwest, southwest, and others of this sort represent compass points.

1. A one-time candidate for the nation's presidency once advised young men to grow with the country by going_____.

2. Columbus and others like him believed they could reach the _____ by sailing _____.

3. Coronado, in 1542, explored much of the American _____.

4. Gold rushes in 1849 and 1859 hastened the settlement of the _____.

5. Explorers Cabot, Cartier, Hudson, and Verrazano unsuccessfully sought the _____ Passage.

6. Molasses from the _____ Indies once served as the basis of the New England rum industry.

7. _____ Carolina was the first state to leave the Union during the Civil War era.

8. _____ Virginia broke with Virginia over the question of secession.

9. At one time in U.S. history the _____ and _____ referred to the two warring factions of the nation.

10. The states of Ohio, Indiana, and Illinois were all carved from the _____ Territory.

11. Jay Cooke financed the building of the _____ Pacific Railroad from Lake Superior to Portland, Oregon. (Better add an "ern" to a direction for this one.)

12. Explorers such as George Weymouth and John Knight were sponsored by the _____ India Company.

13. In 1810 the Republic of _____ Florida was established on land taken from Spain.

14. As a result of Andrew Jackson's Seminole campaign

_____ Florida was brought under United States military control.

15. The famous Gadsden Purchase was made in part to provide a desirable route for the _____ Pacific Railroad. (Another "ern" if you please.)

16. The defense of _____ Korea cost many American lives.

17. One of the most famous airlifts in the world's history came as a result of American determination to supply _____ Berlin when it was blockaded by the Communists in 1948 and 1949.

18. On April 4, 1949, the _____ Atlantic Treaty was signed, becoming a bulwark against aggression and the spread of communism.

19. The Battle of the _____ Atlantic began before the United States had entered World War II.

20. On July 11, 1676, the Quintipartite Deed created_____ _____ and _____ Jersey.

Colleges and Universities of America

A major factor contributing to the high standard of living in the United States is the educational system. There follow very brief descriptions of some points of interest connected with colleges and universities of America. Score yourself on a two-point basis. If you can supply the name of the educational institution described, give yourself one point. If you can give its location by city and state, add another point. Twenty points correct, and you merit a diploma. Eighteen or nineteen points, and you are well on your way to becoming a good student of history. Thirteen to seventeen points places you in the middle of the average American classification. A lesser score, and we all know that you haven't paid careful attention to your history lessons in the past.

Page 212 will educate you concerning our places of higher learning.

1. This campus was the scene of a fierce battle during the Revolutionary War.

2. This university was begun as an academy by Benjamin Franklin.

3. Founded in 1636, this great university was given its name as the result of a gift of four hundred books and £779 from a dying man.

4. This college was the first in the nation to admit women.

5. A Civil War general became president of this university on August 4, 1865. His name is now part of the name of this great university.

6. This college, founded in 1693, and named for the British rulers at that time, is the second oldest college in the United States.

7. The first president of this college was the great educator Horace Mann.

8. A chain stretched across a river is closely associated with the history of this institution of learning.

9. When King George II granted the charter to this center of learning, it was known as King's College.

10. At this institution for higher education may be seen the crypt of John Paul Jones as well as stained glass memorials to David G. Farragut, David D. Porter, and William T. Sampson.

Man, the Builder

Over the years there has been assembled in the United States and over the world a fascinating collection of things built for usefulness or as ornamental symbols of remembrance. All these things stand as monuments to their builders. They often become household words to us in a relatively short time. With only a few exceptions the following items are well known to all Americans; therefore, their identification should be a snap. In fact, a score of seventeen is only average. It takes eighteen or nineteen to be rated as good and very good, while a score of twenty makes you an expert on man-made wonders of the American people.

97

Page 213 will resolve any difficulties which arise from working the quiz. It might be interesting to use a few of the facts below to impress your friends sometime in the near future.

1.   The world's tallest office building reaches 1,472 feet into the sky. What is its name?

2.   The tallest dam in the United States is 726 feet high. Can you name it?

3.   What is the name of the world's tallest masonry structure? It stands 555 feet, 5⅛ inches high.

4.   Name the world's longest cable suspension bridge. It has a main span of 4,260 feet.

5.   Can you give the name of America's largest passenger ship which is 990 feet in length and weighs 44,893 tons?

6.   What is the name of the world's largest refracting telescope, and where is it located? Its lens diameter is 40 inches.

7.   What is America's largest work of sculpture called?

8.   In the 1880's France gave the U.S. a copper statue 151 feet tall. What is it called today?

9.   The United States government once built a 51.2 mile shipping aid outside the continental United States. Can you name it?

10.   In 1942, at a cost of $110,000,000, the United States built a military highway 1,523 miles long. What is it called?

11.   Part of a 2,342 mile waterway was opened in 1959 to carry salt water fleet traffic to inland fresh water ports. What was the recently opened portion of this vast waterway called?

12.   Can you name the world's highest auto suspension bridge? It swings 1,053 feet above the Arkansas River.

13.   What is the name of the world's largest office building which covers 34 acres?

14.   Can you name a structure near Fargo, North Dakota, that is 2,069 feet high?

15.   What is the world's largest reflecting telescope called? Its lens is 200 inches across.

16.   The longest ship ever built is 1,123 feet in length. What is its name?

17. The nation's largest water storage reservoir is located on the Colorado River between Arizona and Nevada. It has a capacity of 32,471,000 acre feet of water. What is it called?

18. Can you tell which university has the nation's largest college stadium? It seats 100,000 spectators.

19. The world's busiest airport is located in the United States. It serves 17 major airlines, 4 local service airlines, 3 cargo carrier lines, and 1 air taxi line. Where is it, and what is its name?

20. A reinforced concrete monument, 570 feet high, commemorating a noted battle fought on April 21, 1836, stands in Texas. The battle won independence for Texas. What is the name of the monument?

Inventors and Their Inventions

Invention, as much as any one thing, has played a significant part in making America great. It is far beyond the scope of any book, much less this one, to trace the history of American invention and do justice to the topic. Sensing that we couldn't write such a history, we have settled for twenty-five inventions which have had a major effect on some aspect of history or which were of more than passing interest.

In the first column we will give you the name or names of the inventors. In the second will be the inventions followed by the date usually associated with their beginnings. Now if you know when these various inventors lived, you can match dates, and the quiz won't be hard at all. If this is not the case, however, you have will to call on your memory and drag forth some all but forgotten facts which will enable you to be a winner on this quiz.

It only takes fifteen correct matches to pass, but who wants to just pass? Let's shoot for eighteen which is a good average score. If you have more ambition, why not try for twenty-two which is well above average, or even for twenty-four which is outstanding. A perfect score is too good to be true; so we won't believe you even if you do make the grade.

Page 213 will either elate or discourage you.

1.	Joseph F. Glidden	A.	Lightning rod—1752
2.	Elias Howe	B.	First American submarine
3.	Lewis Waterman		—1775
4.	George Westinghouse	C.	Bifocal spectacles—1783
5.	Charles Thurber	D.	Steamboat invented—
6.	Orville and Wilbur		1785–87
	Wright	E.	Cotton gin—1793
7.	Oliver F. Winchester	F.	Interchangeable parts—
8.	Walter Hunt		1800
9.	Benjamin Franklin	G.	First successful steamboat
10.	Benjamin Franklin		—1807
11.	George M. Pullman	H.	Reaper—1831
12.	Robert Fulton	I.	Revolver—1835
13.	David Bushnell	J.	Vulcanization of rubber—
14.	Peter C. Hewitt and F. B.		1839
	Crocker	K.	Typewriter—1843
15.	George Eastman	L.	First practical telegraph—
16.	Eli Whitney		1844
17.	Eli Whitney	M.	Sewing machine—1845
18.	Charles Goodyear	N.	Modern safety pin—1849
19.	Cyrus H. McCormick	O.	Repeating rifle—1860
20.	Thomas A. Edison	P.	Sleeping car—1864
21.	Thomas A. Edison	Q.	Air brake—1868
22.	Samuel F. B. Morse	R.	Barbed wire marketed—
23.	John Fitch		1874
24.	Samuel Colt	S.	Telephone—1876
25.	Alexander Graham Bell	T.	Phonograph—1878
		U.	Electric light bulb—1879
		V.	First successful roll film
			patented—1880
		W.	Fountain pen—1884
		X.	Airplane—1903
		Y.	First successful helicopter
			—1918

Was History Like This?

Many people claim that history is a riddle to them. Especially for those people (though anyone may play) we have gathered the riddles which follow. Most of them came to us via our fifth- and eighth-grade students; so they shouldn't be too difficult to answer.

If your wits aren't enough for the task, turn to page 213.

1. If April showers bring May flowers, what do May flowers bring?
2. Why did the old Confederate take his rifle to the ball park?
3. What bus crossed the Atlantic?
4. What made Francis Scott Key famous?
5. Why is the President of the U.S. like the "Star-Spangled Banner?"
6. When did George Washington first ride in a taxi?
7. What do American bald eagles have that no other bird has?
8. Where was the Declaration of Independence signed?
9. What train should Harry Truman and Dwight Eisenhower ride?
10. Why did Eisenhower move to a farm in Pennsylvania?

If you answered all of the above correctly, it is obvious that you spend too much time playing games.

History in Code

Here we have five statements which have become bywords in American history. The only reason you may fail to recognize them is that they have become a bit jumbled in writing. In fact they are written in code. In order to decode them simply use your powers of observation and reason, and determine what letter is represented by each letter in our code. Page 19 will give you some advice if you have never done this sort of thing, and page 103 will provide you with a bit more practice at breaking codes.

We've given you the answers on page 214, but don't be in too great a hurry to turn to the answer page. A bit of thinking will be good for you.

1. "XTU AEYC XTRES VU TNFU XA HUNM RJ HUNM RXJUYH."

    H. B. MAAJUFUYX

2. "TBNC ALBCZ IHO AZSZH MZICA IPB BNC TI-EUZCA WCBNPUE TBCEU BH EUDA LBHED-HZHE...."

    I. FDHLBFH

3. "SO BXO WOUWHO UC BXO TRJBOE YBIBOY...."

    MURYBJBTBJUR

4. "TUAX BX ZUA NPCSOA PJ UCWDX AKAXZO...."

    LANIDSDZBPX PJ BXLAQAXLAXNA

5. "KFC LO GA MTFB, TFB JZK LO GA RCT."

    MKFHOCMMKZ

Mightier Than the Sword

No student of history can doubt the impact certain pieces of literature have made upon the course of a nation. Some have contributed to a change in government, others to a social change, and yet others have merely pointed at the world in protest or in condemnation. It would be impossible to say just which writing has had the greatest effect on the American way of life. With this in mind we have selected the following representative works of American literature and challenge you to match them with their authors. We have included the printing date as an interesting sidelight along with the book or document title.

If you need help, page 214 will provide it.

1. *New England Primer,* c. 1690
2. *Poor Richard's Almanac,* 1732–57
3. *Common Sense,* 1776

4. The Declaration of Independence, 1776
5. *The Federalist*, 1787–88
6. *Uncle Tom's Cabin*, 1852
7. *Progress and Poverty*, 1879
8. *Looking Backward*, 1888
9. "The Significance of the Frontier in American History," 1893
10. *Sister Carrie*, 1900
11. *The Octopus*, 1901
12. *The Pit*, 1903
13. *The Jungle*, 1906
14. *Main Street*, 1920
15. *The Sound and the Fury*, 1929
16. *The Grapes of Wrath*, 1939

And here are the authors:
Alexander Hamilton, John Jay, and James Madison
William Faulkner
Frank Norris (Use twice)
Harriet Beecher Stowe
Sinclair Lewis
Henry George
Thomas Jefferson, John Adams, Benjamin Franklin
Thomas Paine
Upton Sinclair
Frederick Jackson Turner
Edward Bellamy
Benjamin Harris
Theodore Dreiser
John Steinbeck
Benjamin Franklin

Battle Cryptograms

Many of our most famous quotations from history have come to be during the heat of battle. We have selected half a dozen of these well-known quotations for you to identify for author and place spoken. Oh yes, we have placed these messages in code in the best military manner so that your task won't be overly simple.

You may want to turn back to page 19 where our game of "Codes" gives additional instructions for dealing with problems of this sort. All you really need to do to decode these historic statements is to determine what letter each letter in the coded messages represents and break down our code letter by letter.

For those who give up, we have the answers on page 214, but it is considered in the worst of taste to peek.

1. "EPO'U GJSF VOUJM ZPV TFF UIF XIJUFT PG UIFJS FZFT."
   DPMPOFM XJMMJBN QSFTDPUU BU CVOLFS IJMM
2. "XNT LZX EHQD VGDM QDZCX, FQHCKDX."
   BNLLNCNQD FDNQFD CDVDX ZS LZMHKZ AZX
3. "ABCD EFG EHIJGAHGK! . . . QH BFGBA."
   BACOIBN ABPOA QNBKQHR LBIIBQME OD CHSONG SBT
4. "WMC'H USFV GL HTV ITSL."
   XZLHZSC RZOVI PZEJVCXV ZYMZJW HTV XTVIZLVZQV MGHISWV YMIHMC TZJYMJ
5. "Z YCXD TGV KDV MDFET VG SZFYV."
   HCRVCZT WGYT RCEI WGTDA GT MGTYGQQD BZHYCBJ GPP AHGVICTJ
6. "AFCG HAJ LFNH! M BO PFOMIE!"
   DMCCMBO HJPQOKJA KAJNOBI BH BCCBHFFIB RBKK, EJFNEMB

Now why not construct a few cryptograms of your own to confuse your friends?

Quotable Quotes

There have been a number of great and lasting quotations which have come from the lips of Americans. If one were to assemble a number of quotations by one individual, it is quite probable that much of the character of that person would appear through these quotations. We are not suggesting that one can do a character study from the quotations we have selected for your pleasure, but we do suggest that some idea of the character of the men whose names follow a given quotation should serve as a clue to the identity of the speaker. In each instance only one of the three names following the quotation is considered to be the correct source for that quotation.

Should you incorrectly identify one or two quotations, you are still at the head of the class. Three to five errors still rates as above average. Up to ten mistakes is not really too bad, but over fifteen mistaken selections might suggest that you do too little reading concerning those who have made history.

Correct choices may be found on page 215.

1. "I have not yet begun to fight."
   a. George Washington
   b. Patrick Henry
   c. John Paul Jones
2. "All I know is just what I read in the papers."
   a. Calvin Coolidge
   b. Will Rogers
   c. Samuel Goldwin
3. "We must all hang together, or assuredly we shall all hang separately."
   a. Benedict Arnold
   b. Benjamin Franklin
   c. George Rogers Clark
4. "It must be a peace without victory."
   a. Woodrow Wilson
   b. Harry Truman
   c. Abraham Lincoln
5. "Remember the Alamo!"
   a. Zachary Taylor
   b. Sidney Sherman
   c. Robert E. Lee

6. "I never met a man I didn't like."
   a. Woodrow Wilson
   b. Will Rogers
   c. Abraham Lincoln
7. "You may fire when ready, Gridley."
   a. George Dewey
   b. Thomas Jackson
   c. David Farragut
8. "A House divided against itself cannot stand."
   a. William Seward
   b. Abraham Lincoln
   c. Daniel Webster
9. "Damn the torpedoes! . . . go ahead!"
   a. George Dewey
   b. David Farragut
   c. Chester Nimitz
10. "Nuts!" (This was a reply to a German major and captain who brought an ultimatum from their commander, demanding surrender of men trapped for seven days at Bastogne.)
    a. Douglas MacArthur
    b. Dwight David Eisenhower
    c. Anthony Clement McAuliffe
11. "Lafayette, we are here."
    a. Thomas Jefferson
    b. Charles Stanton
    c. Ethan Allen
12. "With malice toward none; with charity for all."
    a. Thomas Jefferson
    b. Abraham Lincoln
    c. Benjamin Franklin
13. "And like the old soldier . . . , I now close my military career and just fade away."
    a. Samuel Houston
    b. Douglas MacArthur
    c. George Marshall

14. "Liberty and Union, now and forever, one and insepa-
    rable."
    a. Abraham Lincoln
    b. George Washington
    c. Daniel Webster

15. "This is the place!"
    a. Douglas MacArthur
    b. Brigham Young
    c. Harriet Beecher Stowe

16. "Speak softly and carry a big stick."
    a. Franklin D. Roosevelt
    b. Theodore Roosevelt
    c. Harry Truman

17. "Four score and seven years ago. . . ."
    a. Thomas Jefferson
    b. Abraham Lincoln
    c. James Madison

18. "I shall return."
    a. Franklin D. Roosevelt
    b. Douglas MacArthur
    c. Dwight David Eisenhower

19. "In a smoke-filled room in some hotel. . . ."
    a. Harry Daugherty
    b. Warren G. Harding
    c. Rutherford B. Hayes

20. "Genius is one per cent inspiration and ninety-nine per
    cent perspiration."
    a. Henry Ford
    b. Harry Firestone
    c. Thomas Alva Edison

21. "Our Federal Union—it must be preserved."
    a. Daniel Webster
    b. Andrew Jackson
    c. Abraham Lincoln

22. "There is no right to strike against the public safety by anybody, anywhere, any time."
    a. Eugene V. Debs
    b. Calvin Coolidge
    c. Franklin Roosevelt

23. "We have met the enemy, and they are ours."
    a. Oliver Hazard Perry
    b. Theodore Roosevelt
    c. Omar Bradley

24. "The business of America is business."
    a. Samuel Gompers
    b. Henry Ford
    c. Calvin Coolidge

25. "Early to bed and early to rise, makes a man healthy, wealthy, and wise."
    a. Henry Ford
    b. Gouverneur Morris
    c. Benjamin Franklin

26. "Yesterday, December 7, 1941—a date which will live in infamy. . . ."
    a. Franklin Roosevelt
    b. Joseph Stilwell
    c. Cordell Hull

27. "The world must be made safe for democracy."
    a. Franklin Roosevelt
    b. Woodrow Wilson
    c. Harry Truman

28. "Truth is generally the best vindication against slander."
    a. Abraham Lincoln
    b. Benjamin Franklin
    c. John C. Calhoun

29. "There's a sucker born every minute."
    a. Samuel Goldwin
    b. P. T. Barnum
    c. Harry Daugherty

30. "See, there is Jackson, standing like a stone-wall."
    a. Robert E. Lee
    b. George B. McClellan
    c. Bernard Bee

31. "This strategy would involve us in the wrong war, at the wrong place, at the wrong time, and with the wrong enemy."
    a. Douglas MacArthur
    b. Harry Truman
    c. Omar Bradley

32. "The only good Indians I ever saw were dead."
    a. Phil Sheridan
    b. Ulysses S. Grant
    c. John C. Frémont

33. "My hat's in the ring."
    a. Lyndon Johnson
    b. Theodore Roosevelt
    c. William Howard Taft

34. "Tin horn politicians."
    a. Charles A. Lindbergh
    b. William Allen White
    c. William Randolph Hearst

35. "One country, one constitution, one destiny."
    a. Daniel Webster
    b. Abraham Lincoln
    c. Henry Clay

36. "It is our true policy to steer clear of permanent alliances with any portion of the foreign world."
    a. James Monroe
    b. George Washington
    c. Thomas Jefferson

37. "All dressed up, with nowhere to go."
    a. William Allen White
    b. Will Rogers
    c. William Randolph Hearst

38. "Let me now . . . warn you in the most solemn manner against the baneful effects of the spirit of party."
   a. Benjamin Franklin
   b. George Washington
   c. Robert E. Lee

39. "Millions for defense, but not one cent for tribute."
   a. James Madison
   b. Charles Cotesworth Pinckney
   c. Robert Livingston

40. "A wise man does not try to hurry history."
   a. John F. Kennedy
   b. Eleanor Roosevelt
   c. Adlai Stevenson

America's Religious History

Religious freedom brought many of the early settlers to the American shores. All too often, however, those who came to escape religious persecution were in turn guilty of the same intolerance toward members of other faiths as they themselves had suffered in the past. Our forefathers both suffered and inflicted death, torture, imprisonment, and general persecution in the name of religion. Established religions have grown to greatness in America, and new faiths have been born here—some to prosper and some to die.

From the religious history of the United States have come to us the names of many leaders. Some had great followings; some were followed by few, but all were sincere. When you have completed your identification of the sixteen religious leaders described below, you will find that the letters marked with an "X," if written in the order in which they appear, spell two words which tell the one thing these sixteen people had in common.

Just in case your knowledge of religious history is too shaky for the task before you, we have provided answers on page 215.

1. __ __ X __ __   __ __ __ __ __   __ __ __ __

The author of *Science and Health with Key to the Scriptures* was the founder of the practice of Christian Science.

2. _ _ _ _   _ _ _ _ _ _ _ _ _ _
      X

In 1638, this religious leader was banished from the Massachusetts Bay Colony because she disagreed with the Puritan philosophy.

3. _ _ _ _ _   _ _ _ _ _ _ _ _ _
                 X

This man fled the Puritan religion and established Rhode Island as a religious haven.

4. _ _ _ _ _ _ _   _ _ _ _
   X

In lieu of payment of a debt, this Quaker accepted a vast tract of wooded land which was later named for him.

5. _ _ _ _ _ _ _   _ _ _ _ _
      X

This Mormon leader led his people to the valley of the Great Salt Lake.

6. _ _ _ _ _ _   _ _ _ _ _ _
            X

The establishment of the Walla Walla, Washington mission was accomplished by this man shortly after leading the first expedition containing women to cross the Rockies in 1836.

7. _ _ _ _ _ _   _ _ _ _ _ _
   X

Son of a noted Puritan clergyman and writer, this Boston religious leader was a noted leader in the persecution of "witches" in the Salem, Massachusetts, witch trials in 1693.

8. _ _ _ _ _ _   _ _ _ _ _ _
           X

A National League ballplayer for eight years, this evangelist reached great heights as a revivalist in the early twentieth century. In 1880, while playing for Chicago, he is credited with originating the term "charley horse" for a pulled muscle.

9. _ _ _ _ _ _   _ _ _ _ _
   X

111

The *Book of Mormon* was based upon the revelations of this man who was later lynched by a mob while held in jail in 1844.

10. __ __ __ __ __   __ __ __ __ __ __ __
                                            X

A noted Senate chaplain, this religious leader is known to millions as "A Man Called Peter."

11. __ __ __ __ __ __ __   __ __ __ __ __ __
    __ __ __ __ __
                X

A noted spiritual writer in the world of today, this man is perhaps best known for *The Power of Positive Thinking*.

12. __ __ __ __ __   __ __ __ __ __ __
                    X

The evangelistic successes of this man reveal an overwhelming present-day interest in and need for religion. His revivals in postwar Western Europe have made him a favorite among modern Europeans.

13. __ __ __ __ __   __ __ __ __
                            X

__ __ __ __ __ __ __

The sister of this antislavery religious leader wrote *Uncle Tom's Cabin*.

14. __ __ __ __ __ __ __   __ __ __ __ __ __ __
                        X

__ __ __ __ __

Perhaps the high point, religiously, in the life of this evangelist-politician came in 1925, in the trial of John Scopes who was charged with teaching evolution in the Tennessee schools.

15. __ __ __ __ __ __ __ __
    __ __ __ __ __ __ __ __
                        X

The Separatists, of whom this man was a leader, are better known to us as Pilgrims.

16. __ __ __ __ __ __   __ __ __ __ __ __
                    X

Yet another person to disagree with the Puritans of the Massachusetts Bay Colony settled at Hartford, Connecticut, in 1636.

Military Leaders in Disguise

If you have forgotten how to play the game "Disguises," check for instructions on page 24. Remember that we hide a name in a sentence among the words of the sentence. As an aid to success we have provided a factual clue following each sentence containing a disguised name. Try to locate the hidden name without use of the clue, but use the clue before giving up.

A perfect score shouldn't be too hard to achieve if you are a born sleuth. Less than twelve correct answers entitles you to a second try. Fifteen to seventeen shows good eyesight and knowledge of our military tradition, while a higher score is just that much better than average.

Page 215 will give you the word, should you need aid.

1. The rain came so hard I could hardly see well enough to drive.
He led one of Lee's three major corps at Gettysburg.

2. As we watched, the dog ran through the sprinkler.
This general took Vicksburg.

3. Joe had trouble eating after having his tonsils out.
Lincoln personally asked this man to lead Union forces.

4. When you visit George and Pat tonight, give them my regards.
He fought in World War II.

5. Remember to put name, address, and phone number on all the application forms you write.
History tells us this man once followed a wolf into a cave.

6. Drive four nails per shingle when putting up the new roof.
In 1918, all Americans knew his name.

7. When you pack the car trunk, why must you always bury the jack so no one can find it if it is needed?
This general of the Confederacy led the "foot cavalry" into battle.

8. As we waded through the marsh, all of us got muddy.

His report was one major cause we stopped supplying Nationalist China.

9. Estelle sees her manager every day about an acting job.

We have been told that Southerners still resent this Union general.

10. Because my family likes her, I dance with Cynthia at every prom.

This Union cavalry officer also served in the West.

11. If it hails, cotton plants may be badly damaged.

He distinguished himself in the war with Mexico.

12. If you let your little pup err, you may have to pay a fine.

A great naval figure, this man was important in the Far East in years past.

13. If the party gives me adequate support, I will win the election.

Gettsyburg was his high point.

14. Will you please call Mr. Long's Tree Trimming Service and have them remove those dead branches from the old maple?

He did not agree with Lee that Pickett should make his historic charge at Gettysburg.

15. Is our old red barn older than the house?

A monument was erected to this man's boot.

16. Is this the way newly rebuilt engines always sound?

His courage bordered on madness.

17. Please pop every bit of the popcorn so we can string it for the Christmas tree.

With this man, Stuart once traded a coat for a hat.

18. What happened to Hal's eye?

This World War II admiral was better known by his nickname than by his first name.

19. What is the oldest kingdom in the world?

He commanded the U.S. Fleet in 1941.

20. David's excellent report erased any doubt of his ability as a student.

He captured or destroyed over forty merchant ships and whalers during the War of 1812.

Noted American Homes

America has thousands of historic homes. We have selected a number of historic and fascinating homes for you to match with their owners. These are all widely known homes belonging to well-known people; therefore, you shouldn't encounter any real difficulty in completing the quiz.

A person really interested in historic places will easily score a perfect set of matched pairs. Fifteen or more correct pairs is good, and a dozen is average. Ten will just pass you; so better score higher.

Page 215 will give our answers.

1.	Mount Vernon	Henry Ford
2.	Monticello	Franklin Roosevelt
3.	The Hermitage	Theodore Roosevelt
4.	Red Hill	Calvin Coolidge
5.	The Breakers	Andrew Jackson
6.	Fair Lane	John D. Rockefeller
7.	Biltmore	James Madison
8.	Peacefield	Patrick Henry
9.	Hyde Park	George Washington
10.	Arlington	Cornelius Vanderbilt
11.	Ashland	George W. Vanderbilt
12.	Gettysburg	James Monroe
13.	Kykuit	Dwight D. Eisenhower
14.	Montpelier	Robert E. Lee
15.	The Beeches	Home of the President of the United States
16.	Oak Hill	Henry Clay
17.	Sagamore Hill	John Adams
18.	The White House	Thomas Jefferson

Biography Detection

Here is a quiz to sharpen your wits. We have chosen some people whose lives and work have had a direct effect on the American way of life. Usually we are interested in only their last name, though in a few cases we'll ask you to supply both first and last names. After each set of blanks signifying a name, you will find a set of two or three clues. The last clue tells you something of the identity of the name you are seeking. The other clues give you a hint of what some of the letters in the name are and where they fit in the name. The numbers below the blanks in the name tell you where to begin writing the word you have discovered to be a part of the name. We don't, however, tell you how long the clue word is because that would be just too much help.

This can be great fun as a timed contest for a group. In that case, you would want to make up a series of your own puzzles to add to these. A little imagination and interest in biography can combine to produce some really good puzzles of this sort.

Should you get stuck, page 216 will help.

A. __ __ __ __ __ __ __ __
   1   2
1. A cut of cured pork
2. __ or off
3. He was America's first Secretary of the Treasury.

B. __ __ __ __ __ __ __ __ __ __ __ __
   1   2
1. "Go _____, young man!"
2. White _____ is the traditional name for the home of the American Presidents.
3. He invented the air brake.

C. __ __ __ __ __ __
   1   2
1. A girl's name
2. Twenty hundred weight
3. This World War II American general was nicknamed "Blood and Guts."

D. __ __ __ __ __ __ __ __ __ __ __
   1   2

1. Left after burning
2. Two thousand pounds
3. He has been called "The Father of His Country."

E. __ __ __ __ __ __ __
   1

__ __ __ __ __ __ __ __ __
   2

1. Opposite of lose
2. Building connected with religion
3. During World War II he was British Prime Minister.

F. __ __ __ __ __ __ __ __ __
     1   2

1. The fall of night—Adam and _____
2. The _____ of the free
3. He was the only American President to serve two terms not in succession.

G. __ __ __ __ __ __ __ __
   1   2

1. A fish or an abbreviation for Grand Army of the Republic
2. "In Flanders _____"
3. He was the second American President to be assassinated.

H. __ __ __ __ __ __ __ __
     1

__ __ __ __ __ __ __ __
    2

1. "Give me liberty ____ give me death!"
2. To protect someone
3. He was a famous mayor of New York City.

I. __ __ __ __ __ __ __ __ __ __ __
   1   2

1. American name for the automobile
2. Preposition showing location—he's ____ the top of the list.

3. This woman anti-saloon agitator raided bars with her hatchet.

J. _ _ _ _ _ _ _ _ _ _ _ _ _
           1   2

1. Method of propelling a boat
2. The relation of John Q. Adams to John Adams
3. He was the American President during World War I.

K. _ _ _ _ _ _
       1

1. Hearing organ
2. His name is at the head of a powerful newspaper syndicate.

L. _ _ _ _ _ _ _ _ _ _ _ _
       1   2

1. A slang term for a poor actor—a cut of pork
2. Past participle of lie (recline)
3. This British Prime Minister, who strove for "peace in our time," was succeeded by Churchill.

M. _ _ _ _ _ _ _ _
      1   2

1. A great distance
2. Piece of scrap cloth
3. The rank of vice admiral was created for him after the Battle of Mobile Bay.

N. _ _ _ _ _ _ _ _ _ _ _ _
      1   2

1. Sick
2. To turn away a blow
3. He was responsible for the purchase of Alaska in 1867.

For Biographers and Such

We have selected thirty well-known people who actively participated in the making of American history. For each individual we have chosen five clues to aid you in identifying the person to whom the clues refer. In general, the clues become more obvious references to the person as they progress. Thus, the first clue is apt to be harder to connect with the person in question than is the last clue. At least we hope this is true.

The object is, of course, to identify the person as quickly as possible. Thus, the longer it takes to identify the individual, the less points are awarded for the identification. If the first clue gives the person away, award five points. The second clue would be worth only four points, and so on until the fifth clue has a value of only one point.

This scoring pattern may be used to quiz yourself, as a quiz you give another person, or as a group game. No matter whether you decide to use this material as a quiz or as a game, it is a good idea to read all five clues for each person. Not only is this a good way to gain interesting information, but there may be times when the added information may cause one to change his original answer. These thirty groups of facts are only a beginning. If you use this material as a game and enjoy using it, you will doubtless continue to construct more such sets of clues for different people.

1

A. This man commanded the Russian Navy on the Black Sea from 1787 to 1789.

B. This American hero was a Scottish imigrant.

C. He once made the statement, "I have not yet begun to fight."

D. During the Revolutionary War he commanded the *Bonhomme Richard*.

E. His real name was John Paul.

2

A. This noted man opposed James Madison's candidacy for President of the United States in 1808 and opposed our entry into the War of 1812 with Great Britain.

B. President Jackson appointed him Minister to Russia, a post he held for only a month.

C. In 1826, he fought a duel with Henry Clay.

D. He headed the opposition to President John Quincy Adams in the Senate from 1825 to 1827 and in the House from 1827 to 1829.

E. In order to distinguish himself from others of the same name he signed his name _____ _____ of Roanoke.

3

A. This famous soldier and statesman was governor of Tennessee from 1827 to 1829.

B. At one time he was adopted into the Cherokee nation.

C. He became commander in chief of the Texas Army in 1835.

D. He avenged the Texas deaths at the Alamo when he defeated the Mexican general Santa Anna at San Jacinto on April 21, 1836.

E. His nickname was "the Raven."

4

A. In 1915, this famous American woman was president of the International Congress of Women at the Hague.

B. She received the Nobel Peace Prize in 1931.

C. She was an active crusader against war.

D. This woman did much work toward improving life in the Chicago slums.

E. In 1889 she founded the famous settlement house known as Hull House.

5

A. During the Civil War this man was radically opposed to slavery.

B. In 1872, he was presidential candidate for two parties.

C. He was one of the Republican Party founders and supported the nomination of Lincoln.

D. The phrase, "Go West, young man" is usually thought of in connection with him.

E. He edited the *New York Tribune*.

6

A.   This noted American was judge of the Tennessee Supreme Court from 1789 to 1804.

B.   In the 1824 presidential election he received more electorial votes than did any of his three opponents; but when the election was decided in the House, he was defeated.

C.   As major general in the United States Army, he defeated British forces at New Orleans in January, 1815, after the peace treaty had been signed ending the War of 1812.

D.   He was nicknamed "Old Hickory."

E.   During his presidency, which began in 1828, he set up the "spoils system" and the "kitchen cabinet." He defeated the rechartering of the Bank of the United States.

7

A.   He was the son of a noted author and physician.

B.   In 1902, President Theodore Roosevelt appointed him to the United States Supreme Court.

C.   His interpretation of the Constitution led him to his doctrine of "clear and present danger."

D.   He criticized the Sherman Antitrust Act.

E.   He served as a justice of the Supreme Court until he was ninety and was a noted dissenter and leader of the liberal wing of the court.

8

A.   This noted labor leader was an immigrant from England.

B.   During World War I he organized the War Committee on Labor.

C.   He attempted to keep politics and labor separate.

D.   He headed the Cigar Makers' Union.

E.   He formed the A.F. of L. and became its first president.

9

A.   This noted physicist was born in Germany and received much of his education in Switzerland.

B.   In 1921, he received the Nobel Prize.

C.   As a young man he worked in the Swiss Patent Office.

D.   In 1905, this scientist proposed his theory of relativity.

E.   In 1939, he wrote President Roosevelt telling him how important it was for the United States to do research on the atomic bomb.

10

A.   This individual was the son of a Welch miner.

B.   He secured passage of Workman's Compensation and mine safety laws.

C.   He was responsible for the organization of the C.I.O.

D.   In 1946, he called a nationwide coal strike which brought about government seizure of coal mines.

E.   He headed the United Mine Workers for many years.

11

A.   This noted American woman taught school for a time in New Jersey.

B.   During the Civil War she aided the sick and wounded.

C.   After the Civil War she headed the government group searching for missing soldiers.

D.   In both the Spanish American War and the Boer War in Africa she was active in relieving suffering brought about by the wars.

E.   Her efforts brought about the establishment of the American Red Cross in 1881.

12

A.   At one time this man was an Illinois State Supreme Court judge.

B.   He proposed the Kansas-Nebraska Act.

C.   He also proposed a railroad from Chicago to San Francisco.

D.   Due to his short stature he was known as the "Little Giant."

E.   In 1858, he debated with Abraham Lincoln for a senate seat in Illinois.

13

A.   At one time this man was a reporter for a Virginia City, Nevada, newspaper.

B. In 1866, he was a roving correspondent in the Sandwich Isles.

C. His first important book was *Innocents Abroad*, a collection of his travel notes.

D. He was born in Florida, Missouri, and raised in Hannibal, Missouri.

E. Writing under the name Mark Twain, he produced such favorites as *The Adventures of Tom Sawyer* and *The Adventures of Huckleberry Finn*.

14

A. He attended West Point Military Academy.

B. His boyhood was spent in Abilene, Kansas.

C. His book *Crusade in Europe* attracted national attention.

D. He was Supreme Allied Commander heading the Allied invasion of Europe on D-Day.

E. In 1952, he was the successful Republican candidate for the office of President of the United States.

15

A. Soon after graduation from the United States Military Academy he fought the Indians in North Dakota.

B. He served in the Spanish American War.

C. In 1916, he was sent by President Wilson into Mexico in an attempt to capture Pancho Villa.

D. He received the rank of General of the Armies.

E. In World War I he commanded the American Expeditionary Forces in Europe.

16

A. This famous man was born in Edinburgh, Scotland, in 1847 and became an American citizen in 1882.

B. He taught teachers of the deaf in New England in the 1870's.

C. In 1872, in Boston he opened a normal training school.

D. Through his work and inventions he learned much about electrical wave transmission.

E. Between 1884 and 1886, he worked on the invention of wax cylinder records for phonographs.

17

A. He supported many reform movements and opposed capital punishment.

B. In his career as a trial lawyer he defended more than fifty people accused of first degree murder of which only one was executed.

C. He was accused of being an atheist.

D. Perhaps his most famous opponent in court was William Jennings Bryan.

E. Among his best known cases were the defenses of Eugene V. Debs, Leopold and Loeb, and John Scopes.

18

A. He rose to the rank of captain in World War I.

B. In 1934, he was elected to the United States Senate from Missouri.

C. He was head of the senatorial committee investigating the United States' National Defense Program.

D. At the Potsdam Conference he was a representative from the United States.

E. He authorized the dropping of the atomic bomb on Japan.

19

A. He was the tenth Chief Justice of the United States Supreme Court.

B. In 1916, he was the Republican nominee for president.

C. Under Harding and Coolidge he was Secretary of State.

D. The Washington Arms Conference was organized by him.

E. He was twice appointed to the Supreme Court and during his time as Chief Justice successfully opposed Franklin Roosevelt's Supreme Court reorganization plan.

20

A. In 1905, he was graduated from the Naval Academy at Annapolis.

B. During World War I he served as Chief of Staff to the commander of the United States Submarine Fleet.

C. Following Pearl Harbor, he took over the Pacific Fleet.

D. He was responsible for the amphibious landing at Guadalcanal.

E. In 1947, he became a special assistant to the Secretary of the Navy.

21

A. He graduated from West Point with the highest academic record in history.

B. He was Aide-de-Camp to Theodore Roosevelt from 1906 to 1907.

C. During World War I he headed the famed Rainbow Division in Europe.

D. When he took the post in 1919, he was the youngest superintendent in the history of the United States Military Academy.

E. During World War II he was Supreme Allied Commander in the Pacific.

22

A. This famous American woman married a cousin.

B. She will long be remembered as a speaker, writer, and humanitarian.

C. From 1949 to 1952, she served as United States representative to the United Nations.

D. Following her husband's death, she was a leader of the Democratic Party.

E. She aided her husband in his battle with infantile paralysis.

23

A. This famous man was born February 22, 1732.

B. He served as a messenger from Governor Dinwiddie in the French and Indian War.

C. On June 15, 1775, he was chosen commander of the Continental Army.

D. In 1787, he was president of the Constitutional Convention.

E. He is often called by the American people, "The Father of Our Country."

24

A. He died at the Battle of Yellow Tavern.

B. He once captured General Pope's coat which he traded for his own captured hat.

C. Robert E. Lee called him "the Eyes of the Confederate Army."

D. James Ewell Brown is included in his name.

E. This noted general was doubtless the most celebrated cavalry officer of the Civil War.

25

A. He was the first governor of Massachusetts.

B. He was president of the Second Continental Congress.

C. His ship *Liberty* was charged with smuggling.

D. The British were seeking him when they marched to Lexington and Concord.

E. When he signed the Declaration of Independence, he wrote especially large so King George III of England could read the signature without his glasses.

26

A. The "Albany Plan" of union was drafted by him.

B. He was America's ambassador to France from 1776 to 1785.

C. He organized Philadelphia's first fire company.

D. This famous man was a noted statesman, editor, diplomat, scientist, and writer.

E. He wrote *Poor Richard's Almanac.*

27

A. This famous colonial lawyer defended the British soldiers after the Boston Massacre. They were acquitted.

B. With John Jay and Ben Franklin he negotiated the Treaty of Paris of 1783 which officially ended the Revolutionary War.

C. He was minister to Great Britain from 1785 to 1788.

D. He was America's first Vice-President.

E. He is the first member of the only father-son combination ever to reach the presidency of the United States.

28

A. He married the daughter of Thomas Hart Benton, senator from Missouri.

B. In 1856, he became the first Republican candidate for President of the United States, but lost to James B. Buchanan.

C. On the eve of war with Mexico he hoisted the American flag over the Mexican territory of California.

D. At the outbreak of the Civil War this soldier was in charge of the Department of the West as a major general.

E. He is often called "the Pathfinder."

29

A. During the Civil War he was engaged in foreign exchange and gold speculation.

B. In 1869, he won control of the Alabama and Susquehanna Railroad from Jay Gould and Jim Fisk.

C. This man took part in the financing and organization of the United States Steel Corporation.

D. As leader of one of America's major banking houses, he helped stabilize financial conditions during the Panic of 1907.

E. His valuable art collection is now housed in the wing, which bears his name, of the Metropolitan Art Museum.

30

A. He entered Congress in his twenties.

B. At the close of the War of 1812 he was a member of the commission to negotiate peace with Great Britain.

C. Under John Quincy Adams he served as Secretary of State.

D. He was influential in framing the Missouri Compromise, the Compromise Tariff of 1833, and the Compromise of 1850.

E. Three times he was an unsuccessful presidential candidate.

Nicknames of the Great

How many times have you called a friend by the nickname Bob or Pat when their name was really Robert or Patricia? Most of the nicknames that follow describe some attribute of the person or refer to some event in which that person took part. Of course, many have entirely different sources.

If you can correctly supply the name of the person whose nickname we give, you are well versed on the people of America. Up to three errors still places you in the excellent category and strongly suggests you must have done a lot of reading. Four to ten errors takes you from above average to average. Eleven to fifteen errors encloses the below average group, and below this group are those who had better read some good biographies of famous Americans.

Page 216 will answer any unanswered questions.

Good luck, and think hard. You have probably heard of every person whose nickname we list. If you haven't, then it is high time that you do.

1. "Old Hickory"
2. "Stonewall"
3. "The Pathfinder"
4. "Old Tippecanoe"
5. "The Little Magician"
6. "Old Eloquent"
7. "Prince Arthur"
8. "Teddy"
9. "Old Rough and Ready"
10. "The Great Commoner"
11. "Old Put"
12. "Honest Abe"
13. "Old Fuss and Feathers"
14. "Black Jack"
15. "The Rock of Chickamauga"
16. "March King of America"
17. "Little Napoleon"
18. "The Darling of Destiny"
19. "The Rail Splitter"
20. "The Sage of Monticello"
21. "Boy General with the Golden Hair"
22. "Boy Orator of the Platte"
23. "The Great Compromiser"
24. "The Little Giant"
25. "Calamity Jane"
26. "Lemonade Lucy"
27. "The Raven"
28. "Mark Twain"
29. "The Swamp Fox"
30. "Ike"
31. "Uncle Sam"
32. "Little Mac"
33. "The Father of Our Country"
34. "The Fox of Kinderhook"
35. "Unconditional Surrender"
36. "Light-Horse Harry"

37.	"Silent Cal"	41.	"Lucky Lindy"
38.	"The Grey General"	42.	"Mad Anthony"
39.	"Old Bory"	43.	"Mr. Citizen"
40.	"The Great Grey Judge"	44.	"Jeb"

Pairs and Couples

The history of the American nation is filled with famous people and noted items which are ordinarily thought of as pairs or couples. Of the hundreds of such associated pairs we have chosen twenty which should pose no great problem for most people to match correctly. Simply decide which name in the left-hand column is usually associated with a name in the second column.

A perfect set of pairs is to be expected, but we will consider eighteen or nineteen as a satisfactory score. Fifteen to seventeen correct pairs tell us that you haven't paid enough attention to the people and things which make up the American nation. Less than fifteen correct pairs just isn't too good. Page 217 will help you decide which of your answers are correct.

You will probably think of a dozen more pairs while working this quiz and a hundred more if you really set your mind to the task. Why not collect these pairs of people and things to use the next time you need a good quiz?

1.	George	Huck
2.	James	Kaufman
3.	Marquette	Clark
4.	Harry	John
5.	Merrimac	Ira
6.	Priscilla	Jacqueline
7.	Pocahontas	Daffy
8.	Dwight	Martha
9.	Jack	Lewis
10.	Sacco	Serapis
11.	Leopold	Eleanor
12.	Lewis	Dolley

13.	*Bonhomme Richard*	Joliet
14.	Franklin	Hammerstein
15.	George	Bess
16.	Rodgers	Loeb
17.	Hart	Mamie
18.	Dizzy	Vanzetti
19.	Martin	John
20.	Tom	*Monitor*

Great Americans and Their Dogs and Horses

Many great Americans have cherished their animal friends. Birds, goats, dogs, horses, and even an alligator have found their way into the White House as pets. Other pets have found their way onto the battlefield with their owners.

We have chosen six dogs and seven horses whose names at one time or another in American history have been commonly known to millions. In one column are the names of the men with whom these animals are associated. The animals' names are in the second column. Your task is, of course, to match the owner with his dog or horse.

A perfect score marks you as an animal lover, though up to two errors would not fail you. Three or more errors should tell you that you haven't paid enough attention to some really interesting points of history.

Page 217 gives the correct matching.

Dogs and Their Masters

1.	Teddy Roosevelt	Rob Roy
2.	Warren Harding	Skip
3.	Calvin Coolidge	Fala
4.	Franklin Roosevelt	Him and Her
5.	Lyndon B. Johnson	Laddie Boy

Horses of Note and Their Owners

1.	George Washington	Rienzi
2.	Zachary Taylor	Nelson

3.	Robert E. Lee	Old Whitey
4.	Stonewall Jackson	Cincinnatus
5.	Andrew Jackson	Traveller
6.	Phil Sheridan	Truxton
7.	Ulysses S. Grant	Little Sorrel

America's Well-Educated Presidents

Today, more than ever before, we as a people are concerned with education. Though not the entire answer, education is the key to many locked doors. With this in mind we thought it might be interesting to discover something about the education of American Presidents. For instance, we found that nine of the Presidents of the United States did not attend college and that of those who did go to college more went to Harvard than to any other college.

We'll give you a few questions concerning the higher education of American Presidents. See how well you know your presidents.

You will get all the help you need in checking your answers on page 218.

1. Who were the nine Presidents who did not have the benefit of a college education?

2. Which five American Presidents attended Harvard?

3. Three American Presidents went to William and Mary. Who were they?

4. Two Presidents were educated at Princeton. Can you name them?

5. West Point was attended by two Presidents. Which two?

6. The remaining fourteen Presidents attended fourteen different colleges. How many can you identify correctly?

If you didn't score very high on this quiz, don't worry about it. We included it because it was of interest to most people, though a bit rough for a good quiz.

Soldiers in the White House

Twenty American Presidents were at one time or another members of the armed forces. Of course, all of the Presidents have been commander in chief of our military forces as is provided for in the Constitution. It will take a real expert on military history to match the twenty Presidents below with their military exploits. However, most people after a little thought should be able to score seventeen or more correct answers.

When you have fought a good fight with this quiz, check on page 218 for the correct answers.

President

1.	George Washington	11.	Lyndon B. Johnson
2.	Andrew Jackson	12.	Andrew Johnson
3.	Zachary Taylor	13.	Franklin Pierce
4.	Ulysses S. Grant	14.	James Monroe
5.	Theodore Roosevelt	15.	James B. Buchanan
6.	Harry S. Truman	16.	Rutherford B. Hayes
7.	Abraham Lincoln	17.	James A. Garfield
8.	William Henry Harrison	18.	Chester A. Arthur
9.	Dwight D. Eisenhower	19.	Benjamin Harrison
10.	John F. Kennedy	20.	William McKinley

Military History

A. Fought in the Mexican War

B. Reached the rank of major in the Civil War and fought at Antietam, South Mountain, Winchester, and Cedar Creek

C. Commanded a PT boat in the Pacific Theater during World War II

D. Led the Continental Army

E. Served with Winfield Scott in the war with Mexico

F. Served as a captain in World War I

G. Defeated Robert E. Lee in 1865

H. Colonel of the 70th Indiana Regiment which served in Kentucky

I. Left William and Mary College to fight in the Continental Army

J. Commissioned major in the Ohio Volunteers in the Civil War and rose to major general

K. Commanded a Union brigade at Shiloh

L. Was brigadier general of New York State Militia in the Civil War

M. Noted general in the War of 1812

N. As a brigadier general was military governor of Tennessee during much of the Civil War

O. Led Allied forces at D-Day invasion

P. Nicknamed "Rough and Ready" in campaign against Mexican forces

Q. Fought in the Black Hawk War

R. Led famous Rough Riders at San Juan Hill

S. Fought Indians in the battle at Tippecanoe

T. Served as naval officer in World War II and was once decorated by General MacArthur

Wives of the Presidents

The position of First Lady carries with it great responsibilities, for the First Lady is in many ways at the head of the nation, and her actions are a reflection upon the entire country.

Here is a little spelling lesson which should bring some interesting facts to light. The object of this little quiz is to discover the name of the First Lady under discussion and spell her name using clues given concerning her life and things which had a bearing on her life. Simply fill in the blanks found in each clue and use any numbered letters to fill in the corresponding spaces in the spelling of the name of the First Lady. Sounds easy, and it is— as well as fun. Don't stop if you should discover the woman's name near the beginning of the series of clues. Go ahead and complete the clues, as they are often interesting in content and sometimes a test of your wits to complete.

When you have successfully identified these women, you might check your clues and findings with page 218.

1. __ __ __ __   __ __ __ __ __ __
   1 10 7 2   4 3 6 5 9 8

A. While the White House was being remodeled, the President and his wife lived at __ __ __ __ __   __ __ __ __ __
                                              1   2

for three and one half years.

B. Her daughter, __ __ __ __ __ __ __ __, made her
                   5   3   4

debut as a concert singer in 1947 with the Detroit Symphony Orchestra.

C. When in 1934 her husband was elected to the __ __ __ __-
                                                 6

__ __   __ __ __ __ __ __   __ __ __ __ __ __ she served
7   8 9   10

as his secretary.

2. __ __ __ __ __ __ __ __ __ __ __
   15 2 16 14 11 13 1 5 6 8

   __ __ __ __ __ __ __
   17 9 3 7 4 10 12

A. Due to her command of many foreign __ __ __-
                                        1 2 3

__ __ __ __ __ __ this First Lady often greeted visitors to
4

the White House in their native tongue.

B. For a time she worked for the __ __ __ __ __ __ __-
                                             5 6

__ __ __ Times Herald interviewing interesting people.
7

C. During her __ __ __ __ __ __ __ career she __ __ __ __-
                8   9   11

__ __ __ __ at Vassar, the Sorbonne, and George Washington
10

__ __ __ __ __ __ __ __ __ __ __.
      13   12

134

D.   Both she and her husband were well known to "John __
                                                      14
Public." In fact, her husband, John, was affectionately known to
the public by his nickname __ __ __ __.
                           15   16 17

3.   __ __ __ __   __ __ __ __ __ __ __
     8 4 3 7   10 1 11 9 5 2 6
A.   During the tragic era of the __ __ __ __ __   __ __ __
                                   1   2   4 3
this First Lady saw her country divided against itself.
B.   Her oldest __ __ __ was named Robert.
                5 6
C.   Though her husband was elected to two terms of office,
she spent only four __ __ __ __ __ as First Lady, because of
                    7
the untimely death of her husband near the start of his second

__ __ __ __.
      8
D.   The issuing of the Emancipation __ __ __ __ __ __ __ __-
                                      9 10
__ __ __ __ in 1863 was a major step in civil rights legislation
      11
by her husband.

4.   __ __ __ __ __ __   __ __ __ __ __ __ __
     11 10 9 7 12 6   8 5 13 1 2 3 4
A.   When in 1814 the British burned __ __ __ __ __ __ __-
                                      5 2   1
__ __ __, this lady saved many important papers from destruc-
3 4
tion.
B.   She was seventeen __ __ __ __ __ younger than her
                       6
husband and extremely beautiful. She has been called the most
__ __ __ __ __ __ __ __ of American First __ __ __ __ __ __.
7   8   10   9

C. After her husband __ __ __ __ in 1836, she moved back
            11   12 13
to Washington, where she remained a society figure until her
death at the age of eighty-one.

5. __ __ __ __ __ __ __   __ __ __ __ __ __ __ __ __
   12 13 8 4 1 10 11   14 5 9 6 15 7 3 16 2

A. This noted woman served as United States representative
to the __ __ __ __ __ __   __ __ __ __ __ __ __ fol-
          1   2 3   4   5   6
lowing World War II.

B. Her interest in politics became active when her husband
was __ __ __ __ __ __ __ __ __ of New York.
     9 7 8   10 11

C. The most shocking event during her reign as First Lady
was probably the surprise bombing of __ __ __ __ __
                                            12   13
__ __ __ __ __ __ in 1941.
14

D. Her husband was __ __ __ __ __ __ __ __ to the office
                    15 16
of the President of the United States four consecutive times.

6. __ __ __ __ __   __ __ __ __
   4 5 9 8 3   1 2 7 6

A. This First Lady planned for the planting of the cherry trees
around Washington's famous __ __ __ __ __   __ __ __ __ __.
                            1   2   3

B. She was instrumental in founding the Cincinnati Symphony __ __ __ __ __ __ __ __ __.
       4 5   6

C. Her husband was appointed __ __ __ __ __ Justice of
                              7
the Supreme Court in 1921.

D. In 1900, she accompanied her husband to the Philippines
where he served as Governor __ __ __ __ __ __ __.
                             8   9

7. $\overline{}\ \overline{}\ \overline{}\ \overline{}\ \overline{}\ \overline{}\ \overline{}$ $\overline{}\ \overline{}\ \overline{}\ \overline{}\ \overline{}$
   3 11 7 6 5 12 4   10 2 9 8 1

A. This First Lady was both the wife and the mother of an American __ __ __ __ __ __ __ __ __ __.
         1   2

B. Her husband served as United States minister to the European countries of __ __ __ __ __ __ and __ __ __-
                                        3   6
__ __ __ __. Her experiences in these nations aided her when
4 5
she became First Lady.

C. She and her husband were the first couple to live in the
__ __ __ __ __   __ __ __ __ __, even though it was not
      7
entirely __ __ __ __ __ __ __ __ __ when they moved in.
            8

D. The appointment of John __ __ __ __ __ __ __ __ __
                              9   10
as Supreme Court Chief Justice was perhaps the most important single act of her __ __ __ __ __ __ __ while __ __ __ __ __-
                              11   12
__ __ __ __.

8. $\overline{}\ \overline{}\ \overline{}\ \overline{}\ \overline{}\ \overline{}\ \overline{}\ \overline{}$ $\overline{}\ \overline{}\ \overline{}\ \overline{}\ \overline{}\ \overline{}\ \overline{}$
   10 14 4 5 1 11 12 9   8 6 7 2 3 13 15

A. The only American President who was a newspaper
__ __ __ __ __ __ was this lady's husband. He edited the
1 2 3   4 5
Marion, Ohio __ __ __ __.
               6 7

B. When the 1920 Republican convention was deadlocked, her husband was suggested as a "dark __ __ __ __ __" and was
                                          8   9
a successful candidate.

137

C. Her husband's most important achievement as President was the Limitation of Armaments __ __ __ __ __ __ __ __ __ __.
$$\text{13 10}\text{11 12}$$

D. The Teapot Dome __ __ __ scandals caused great
$$\text{14}$$

__ __ __ __ __ to her normally happy husband, who died
15

soon after the scandals were publicly disclosed.

9. __ __ __   __ __ __ __ __ __
$$\text{5 3 4}\text{8 6 7 9 1 2}$$

A. Her husband's profession of __ __ __ __ __ __ __ __ __
$$\text{1 2}$$

took the couple to China in 1899 where he was director general of mines.

B. This charming First Lady was at one time president of the American Girl __ __ __ __ __ __ __.
$$\text{3 4}$$

C. Both she and her __ __ __ __ __ __ __ were __ __-
$$\text{8}$$

__ __ __ __ in relief work in __ __ __ __ __ __, England,
$$\text{9}\text{5 6}\text{7}$$

during World War I.

10. __ __ __ __ __   __ __ __ __ __
$$\text{5 6 4 10 3}\text{1 9 7 2 8}$$

A. Her husband returned from the Civil War a famous

__ __ __ __ __ __ __.
1   2   3 4

B. Just four days before his death on __ __ __ __ 23,
$$\text{5 6}$$

1885, her husband completed the writing of his *Memoirs* which earned $500,000 in __ __ __ __ __ __ __ __ for his widow.
$$\text{7}\text{8}$$

C. Today she rests beside her husband in a tomb on Riverside
__ __ __ __ __ in New York City.
   9 10

Assassination!

On four occasions in American history individuals have taken it upon themselves to attempt to change the government by taking the life of the President.

We have assembled the following quiz to give you a chance to test your knowledge concerning these four tragic events. As you will see, there are seven groups of four dates, names, and places. Your task is to use these groups of four items to put together the information relating to the four assassinations.

After you have finished, you may check yourself on page 219.

Counting one point for each correct placement of a fact, you have a possible score of twenty-eight which is actually above expectations. Over twenty-five is very good, over twenty-two is good, and more than eighteen correct choices is passing.

President

Abraham Lincoln   John F. Kennedy
William McKinley   James A. Garfield

Vice-President Who Succeeded

Chester A. Arthur   Theodore Roosevelt
Lyndon B. Johnson   Andrew Johnson

Date the President Was Shot

July 2, 1881   November 22, 1963
September 6, 1901   April 14, 1865

Date of President's Death

November 22   April 15
September 19   September 14

Place of Shooting

Railroad Station   Parade
Pan-American Exposition   Ford's Theater

139

Assassin's Name

Leon Czolgosz   John Wilkes Booth
Charles J. Guiteau   Lee Harvey Oswald

City in Which President Was Shot

Dallas, Texas   Buffalo, New York
Washington, D.C.   Washington, D.C.

Who Was President When . . . ?

The events which occur during the term of office of any given American President affect the course of history in hundreds of ways, many of which the man-on-the-street little understands. During the terms of all Presidents, however, there have been events which were either well understood or were at least common knowledge to the majority of the people of America, if not the world.

Here are four events associated with the terms of office of some of the Presidents of the United States. If you can identify the President in office during the time the first event occurred, give yourself five points. If you have to read the second event, your score drops to three. The third event limits your score to two; and should you need to study the final event in order to identify the President involved, your score is only one point. Failure to give the correct answer takes five points from your total score; so even though you feel certain of your choice, it might be a good idea to glance at the other clues just to be on the safe side.

A final total of less than fifty points is not passing, while a score of above seventy-five is excellent. Between those points is where most people score. Page 220 will aid in checking your answers.

This one works well for group quizzes. Use it on the basis of a first-hand-up quiz for the group, giving points as suggested above but subtracting five for any wrong answer, no matter how many wrong answers the players give. It will keep the group honest in their guesses and may well shake up the few who end the game on the minus side of the score sheet.

1

A. The Tennessee Valley Authority came into being.

B. The Social Security Act was made law.

C. Pearl Harbor was attacked by the Japanese.

D. The D-Day invasion of Europe took place.

2

A. The A.F. of L. was organized.

B. The Haymarket Riot occurred.

C. The great Pullman strike aroused the nation.

D. The Klondike gold rush began.

3

A. World War I began.

B. The United States entered the war.

C. The Fourteen Points were presented.

D. The Treaty of Versailles was signed.

4

A. Reconstruction of the South was begun.

B. The United States bought Alaska.

C. The Grange became a part of the life of rural America.

D. The President was impeached and acquitted.

5

A. The first political nominating conventions were held.

B. The telegraph was developed.

C. The President vetoed the charter renewal for the Bank of the United States.

D. Texas declared its independence.

6

A. America and Spain went to war.

B. The United States claimed the Hawaiian Islands as our territory.

C. We gained Puerto Rico, Guam, and the Philippines by treaty.

D. The President was assassinated.

7

A. Atomic bombs were dropped on Japan.

B. The United States organized the Berlin airlift.

C. NATO was formed.

D. The United States sent troops to Korea.

8

A. The United States added the Louisiana Purchase to the nation.

B. The Lewis and Clark expedition was undertaken to explore our newly acquired territory.

C. Zebulon Pike explored our western area.

D. The *Clermont* appeared on the Hudson River.

9

A. The Philadelphia-Pittsburgh Turnpike was finished.

B. A treaty with Spain added Florida to the United States.

C. The Missouri Compromise became law.

D. Stephen Austin began settlement in Texas.

10

A. The Department of Health, Education, and Welfare was set up.

B. The Supreme Court ruled against segregated public schools.

C. The A.F. of L. and C.I.O. formed one union.

D. The St. Lawrence Seaway was opened.

11

A. The stock market crashed.

B. Boulder Dam was begun.

C. The Reconstruction Finance Corporation was begun.

D. Hitler took over the rule of Germany.

12

A. America's first transcontinental railroad was finished.

B. Barbed wire was patented, ending the open range.

C. Colorado became the thirty-eighth state.

D. Baseball's National League was organized.

13

A. The War of 1812 was fought.
B. The National Road was begun.
C. The Battle of New Orleans took place.
D. Indiana became the nineteenth state to join the Union.

14

A. Departments of State, Treasury, War were created.
B. Eli Whitney invented the cotton gin.
C. The Bill of Rights was ratified and became a part of the Constitution.
D. Vermont became the fourteenth state to join the Union.

15

A. The Supreme Court handed down the Dred Scott decision.
B. John Brown led a raid at Harper's Ferry.
C. The first oil well was drilled in Pennsylvania.
D. The Confederacy was formed.

16

A. The Pure Food and Drug Act was made law.
B. Orville and Wilbur Wright flew at Kitty Hawk.
C. The I.W.W. was organized.
D. The Federal Meat Inspection Act was passed.

17

A. The Morrill Act for education was passed.
B. The Homestead Act became law.
C. Nevada became a state.
D. The President was assassinated.

Presidential Cross-Up

As can be seen, we have the American Presidents crossed-up all over the page. We'd appreciate it if you would arrange them in their proper places for us. To help you decide where to place each President, we will give you the name of his Vice-President (if he had more than one Vice-President, we will still give you only one).

Below you will find a list of the Presidents of the United States by last name or by last name and first initial when two have the same last name. The way the President's name is written below is the way it will fit into the puzzle.

Again we would like to suggest that you paper clip a thin piece of paper over the page in order not to write in the book. Or better yet, use a piece of squared paper and build your puzzle as you write in the correct names, making sure your pattern follows ours.

Page 220 will solve any problems you may encounter.

Here are the Presidents:

Washington	Fillmore	T. Roosevelt
J. Adams	Pierce	Taft
Jefferson	Buchanan	Wilson
Madison	Lincoln	Harding
Monroe	A. Johnson	Coolidge
J. Q. Adams	Grant	Hoover
Jackson	Hayes	F. Roosevelt
Van Buren	Garfield	Truman
W. Harrison	Arthur	Eisenhower
Tyler	Cleveland	Kennedy
Polk	B. Harrison	L. Johnson
Taylor	McKinley	

Here are your vice-presidential clues:

Across		Down	
2.	Richard M. Johnson	1.	John C. Calhoun
3.	Calvin Coolidge	4.	Schuyler Colfax
6.	Millard Fillmore	5.	Charles W. Fairbanks
10.	John Adams	7.	Hannibal Hamlin
11.	(None)	8.	Chester A. Arthur
12.	Charles Curtis	9.	Levi P. Morton
14.	Charles G. Dawes	10.	Thomas R. Marshall
15.	James S. Sherman	13.	Aaron Burr

(Across, *cont.*)

16. Daniel D. Tompkins
17. Thomas Jefferson

(Down, *cont.*)

15. Alben W. Barkley
19. Richard Nixon

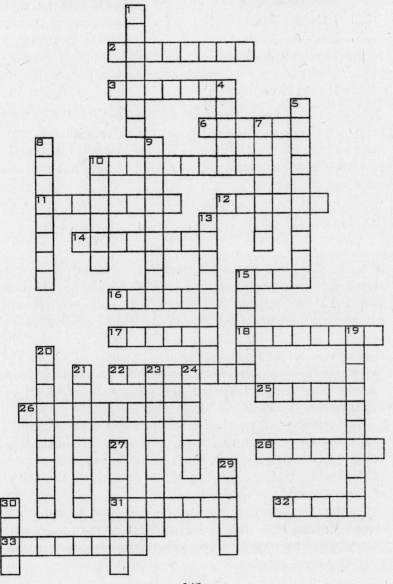

(Across, cont.)	(Down, cont.)
18. Garret A. Hobart	20. John Tyler
22. John C. Breckinridge	21. (None)
25. William R. King	23. Adlai E. Stevenson
26. John N. Garner	24. (None)
28. Elbridge Gerry	27. Martin Van Buren
31. Lyndon B. Johnson	29. William A. Wheeler
32. (None)	30. George M. Dallas
33. Hubert Humphrey	

Sorry about all those Presidents who did not have Vice-Presidents since they themselves left that office vacant when they moved to the office of President. We are sure you will be able to fill in the proper name with just a bit of detective work on your part, however.

Moments from History

Many of the more important moments in history have concerned documents, organizations, court decisions, and the like, as well as actual happenings. This puzzle-quiz is concerned with a number of these items and happenings. The number of blanks, of course, indicates the number of letters required to spell the word or phrase which matches the final clue in each puzzle. The first two or three clues give hints to the letters needed to spell the missing name. These clues are lettered to match the letters beneath various blanks in the blanks representing the answer.

After working this puzzle you will probably enjoy working a similar puzzle dealing with some Americans who have contributed to the development of our nation. It is found on page 115. Page 221, by the way, will give you the answers for this set of puzzles should you need aid.

Constructing puzzles of this type on your own can be fun and a good learning experience as well. When you have a few minutes, why not try your hand at it and pass on some of your creations for others to solve.

1. __ __ __ __ __ __ __ __ __ __ __ __ __
     A   B   C

A. Dried grass used for feeding livestock

B. German monetary unit

C. The ____ Grande forms much of the border between the United States and Mexico.

D. This labor struggle exploded into violence in Chicago, May, 1886.

2. __ __ __ __ __ __ __ __ __ __ __
     A   B

A. Spanish word for saint

B. Past tense of run

C. American city nearly destroyed by an earthquake

3. __ __ __ __ __ __ __ __ __ __ __
           A   B

A. Word indicated something past

B. Anger

C. Mrs. O'Leary's cow kicked over the lantern and started the whole affair.

4. __ __ __ __ __ __ of __ __ __ __ __ __ __
       A   B

A. A violent fever

B. Electrically charged atoms

C. First worldwide attempt at world control of nations— Wilson's Fourteenth Point

5. __ __ __ __ __ __ __ __ __ __ __ __
     A   B

A. One who is for something

B. Contraction of I have

C. Theodore Roosevelt's supporters originated this party in 1912.

6. __ __ __ __ __ __
     A   B

A. What we use to cook in

B. Slang term for mother

C. The only canal connecting the Atlantic with the Pacific crosses this country.

7. __ __ __ __ __   __ __ __ __ __ __ __ __ __
   　　A　　　　　　B　　　　　　　C

A. Beast of burden related to the cow
B. Johnny _____ was a nickname for Confederate soldiers.
C. The king of beasts
D. Chinese revolutionists attempted to expel foreigners from China in 1900.

8. __ __ __ __ __   __ __ __ __ __ __   __ __ __
   　　A　　　　　　　B　　　　　　　　　C

A. "_____ of the free"
B. "_____ for one and one for _____"
C. "_____ well your part, for there all honor lies."
D. Law assuring the purchase of western silver by the federal government—1878

9. __ __ __ __ __ __ __   __ __   __ __ __ __ __
   　　　A　　　　　　　　　　　B

A. Opposite of day
B. Nickname for laboratory
C. Early industrial labor union originated in 1871 by Uriah Stephens

10. __ __ __ __ __ __ vs. __ __ __ __ __ __ __ __ __
    　　　A　　　　　　　　　　　B

A. Opposite of more
B. The eldest _____ usually inherited his father's holdings in early America.
C. Famous Supreme Court decision that upheld segregation of rail facilities in Louisiana

11. __ __ __   __ __ __ __ __   __ __ __
    　　A　　　　　　B　　　　　　　C

A. Opposite of old
B. That part of our planet which is not water
C. The Reclamation _____ of 1902 set aside proceeds from public land sales for irrigation projects in arid areas.

12. __ __ __ __ __   __ __ __ __ __ __ __ __

       A   B   C

A. Abreviation for latitude

B. To fix

C. Adult males

D. Provisions written into the Cuban constitution and the treaty between the United States and Cuba to insure American and Cuban harmony—1901–03—abrogated May 29, 1934

13. __ __ __ __ __ - __ __ __ __ __ __ __ __

       A   B

__ __ __

C

A. Abbreviation for United States ships

B. A piece of glass

C. The scourge of mankind—source of our greatest expense and loss.

D. President Theodore Roosevelt received the Nobel Peace Prize for his work in arranging a settlement between the parties involved in this conflict.

14. __ __ __   __ __ __ __ __ __   __ __

     A   B

__ __ __ __ __ __ __

C

A. A young man

B. It takes three _____ to retire a side in baseball.

C. Abbreviation for meridian

D. Organization for young campers imported from England and incorporated in 1910

15. __ __ __ __ __ __ __ __ __

     A   B

A. Abbreviation for the United States

B. Lifeguards usually have a _____ because of exposure to ultraviolet rays of the sun.

C. Passenger ship sunk by a German submarine off the Irish coast, 1915

16. __ __ __ __ __ __   __ __ __ __ __ __
         A   B

A. Abbreviation for German storm troops in World War II
B. Sporting or honest
C. The sinking of a French cross-channel passenger ship by German submarines caused this disaster.

17. __ __ __ __ __ __ __ __ __ __
         A   B

A. Large rodent usually considered first to leave a sinking ship
B. Exclamation meaning a boo-boo or mistake
C. Troops dropped from planes

18. __ __ __ __ __   __ __ __ __ __
A   B

A. A small, green vegetable related to the bean family
B. "either _____"
C. Organized by President John F. Kennedy to further world peace and understanding through the volunteer efforts of youth

19. __ __ __ __ __ __ __ __
       A   B

A. A hole—"The _____ and the Pendulum"
B. Anger
C. British fighter plane that helped the R.A.F. win the Battle of Britain

20. __ __ __ __—__ __ __ __ __
       A   B

A. Opposite of beginning
B. "A life of _____." "He flies through the air with the greatest of _____."
C. Bill to send supplies to countries fighting fascism

21. __ __ __ __ __ __ __ __ __   __ __ __ __
       A   B

A. Contraction for I am
B. Opposite of woman

C. This message from the German government to Mexico promised Mexico the states of Texas, New Mexico, and Arizona, if she would aid Germany in the event of a war between the United States and Germany—1917.

Word Search

We are going to give you the name of a document of vast importance to all Americans. Then we will give you a number (fifteen to be exact) of definitions. The letters spelling the word to which the definition refers may be found within the name of the document, though not necessarily in the same order. You merely decide on the word defined, sort through the letters spelling the document name until you find those you need, and write the word you have just spelled. (If you need further instructions, check our game of "Search Them Out" on page 40.)

Get your thinking cap on and be ready. A score of ten is passing, twelve is above average, thirteen very good, fourteen excellent, and fifteen indicates you are a detective by profession.

Page 221 will verify your findings.

Here is the name of the document we have been discussing:

Declaration of Independence

1. A famous Revolutionary War general who is now remembered as a traitor (last name)
2. Great Confederate general of the Civil War (last name)
3. Originator of the use of the assembly line (last name)
4. Original inhabitant of the United States
5. America's largest labor organization
6. Historic term describing an armored ship
7. A liquid without which the American nation could not continue to exist as it now does
8. Colonial American who wrote *Common Sense* (last name)
9. First name of the American who developed the idea of interchangeable parts paving the way to future mass production
10. Man-made waterway
11. One-hundredth anniversary of a historic event

151

12. America's most valuable resource other than people

13. At one time this state was known as the Bear Flag Republic.

14. Famous American colonizer who was a Quaker (last name)

15. A sudden fear concerning financial affairs of the nation such as has occurred in 1819, 1837, 1857, 1873, 1893, 1907, and 1929 in the United States

Second Word Search

The only difference in this and our previous "Word Search" is that this quiz is a bit more lengthy and uses a different source word.

You will need eighteen correct responses in order to pass, and twenty in order to reach the average mark. Twenty-two classes you as very good, twenty-four as excellent, and a perfect paper suggests the quiz was too easy.

Page 221 is for those who aren't certain of their answers or who get stuck.

Here are your source words:

United States of America

1. A branch of the armed forces of the United States originally carried on ships for hand-to-hand fighting and landings.

2. Buying and selling between nations

3. The second and sixth American Presidents (last name)

4. The nation with which the United States shares the world's longest unprotected boundary

5. Continent on which are found China, much of Russia, India, and other countries affecting the foreign policy of the United States

6. A counting of the nation's people

7. A famous canal connecting the Great Lakes with the Mohawk River

8. Metal which forms the basis of much of the industry of Pittsburgh, Gary, and Detroit

9. The only state in the Union touching only one other state

10. The crystal set was the parent of this means of nation-wide communication

11. The doctor who is credited with proving the cause of Yellow Fever, enabling the United States to continue work on the Panama Canal (last name)

12. The branch of Congress in which each state has two members.

13. The President of the United States who ordered the use of American forces in the Berlin Airlift of 1948–49 (last name)

14. To restrict free movement of news

15. That branch of American government which interprets the laws

16. Inventor of the phonograph, motion pictures, and the incandescent light (last name)

17. Compulsory military service

18. The chief source of the taxes which finance the American government

19. Powered the *Clermont*

20. The British demanded payment of tax on this item in an attempt to demonstrate their authority to levy taxes on the American Colonists

21. Agreements between nations

22. A name commonly given British sympathizers living in the Colonies during the Revolution

23. Indian tribe which took part in the Meeker Massacre and was later moved by the government to a reservation in Utah

24. Bomb responsible for the end of World War II against Japan

25. Negro slave whose fate was finally decided by the United States Supreme Court (last name)

Links of History

As can be seen from the puzzle diagram, this quiz is a close relative of both the criss-cross and crossword puzzles. When the words of the puzzle have been correctly placed, they will form an interlocking chain. This is in keeping with the fact that events in history do not stand alone but are related to what has gone before and what will follow in the future.

After you have worked this puzzle, why not try building a few of your own? They may be as large or as small as you wish. It is lots of fun to make a chain puzzle about one event in history, such as the Civil War, and have all words in the puzzle related to that event.

When you wish to check your work, turn to page 221.

Across

1. City in which a famous tea party occurred
3. Name for British sympathizer in 1776
4. Lone Star State
6. First name of founder of Rhode Island
7. Mission which served as a fort in 1836
8. The nineteenth American President
10. Married Pocahontas
12. Great leader of the United Mine Workers
14. Confederate commander at the Battle of Winchester
16. Great Confederate cavalry leader
18. Secretary of the Treasury under Harding
20. Wrote of the American West including "The Outcasts of Poker Flat"

Down

1. Hill after which a Revolutionary battle was named
2. One who is born and reared in an area
4. "Old Rough and Ready"
5. Man who brought plans for power spinning machines to America
8. President in office at the beginning of the Great Depression
9. To stop work in demand for better pay, benefits, conditions
11. Founder of American Girl Scouts
12. Body of water on which Macdonough won fame in 1814
13. Powered ships in Revolution
15. ____-Day Saints settled Utah

(Across cont.)

22. KDKA was its first station

(Down cont.)

16. Scene of witch trials

17. Means of transportation which hurt canal business

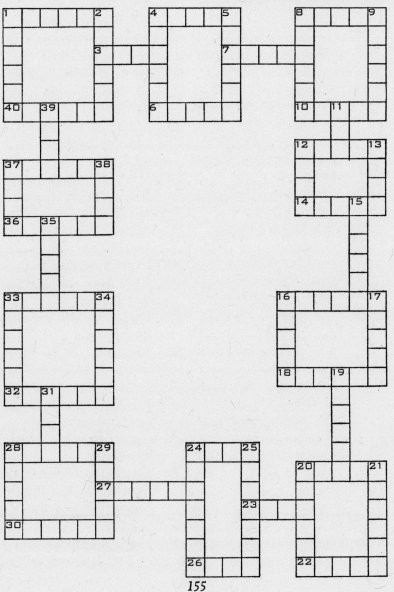

(Across cont.)

23. _____ McHenry's bombardment was witnessed by Francis Scott Key.
24. Socialist labor leader jailed during Pullman strike
26. Seaman hired by English to raid American shipping and later hanged as a pirate
27. Leader of first Texas settlers
28. Means of protecting an invention
30. Nearly deaf inventor
32. Owner of mill where gold was discovered to start the California Gold Rush of 1849
33. Man-made waterways
36. _____ Dome scandal grieved President Harding.
37. Fourteenth American President
40. Silversmith who rode to warn colonists of approaching British troops in 1775

(Down cont.)

19. First name of "Plant Wizard"
20. Leader of Germany during World War II
21. Native of "Seward's Icebox"
24. Scene of mass evacuation of troops early in World War II
25. Owner of Dred Scott at time of Supreme Court decision
28. Wrote *Common Sense*
29. Pen name of Samuel L. Clemens
31. American President who later became Chief Justice of the Supreme Court
33. Last name of Martha's first husband
34. Fort fired on at opening of Civil War
35. Captured Fort Ticonderoga
37. British statesman who felt the Colonies should not be taxed
38. Area Columbus wanted to reach
39. Granted to women by the Nineteenth Amendment

Who, What, When, Where, Why, and How?

Have you ever noticed how many questions begin with one of the words making up the title of this quiz? The seventy-five questions which follow all begin with those six words. Many of the questions ask for commonly known facts as answers. Some will introduce you to little known facts. Quite frankly, one or two are fairly tricky questions.

This quiz makes no claims to being an ordered or orderly approach to history. It just covers the American scene in a rather hit-and-miss fashion, stopping wherever something of interest occurs. It may be used for one of the quiz games suggested earlier in the book, or it may be taken as just a quiz on interesting points in history.

A score of seventy is almost unbelievable and something of which to be proud. Sixty and over would rate one as being rather good at history. Fifty is above average, which is anything above forty. Less than thirty would fail a player, but let's not talk of failure so early in the game.

Disputes among players should be referred to page 222.

1. Why didn't James Buchanan, the fifteenth American President, ever allow his wife to accompany him to social functions in Washington?

2. Why didn't we use the atomic bomb against Germany as well as against Japan?

3. Why does everyone remember Paul Revere, but few know of William Dawes and Samuel Prescott?

4. Why wasn't George Washington ever allowed to live in the White House?

5. Why was Sitting Bull in command of the Sioux instead of Geronimo at the Battle of the Little Big Horn?

6. Why did many canals go out of business after having been used for only a few years?

7. What early American President owned and loved a pet mockingbird?

8. What was the name of the woman who took her husband's place at a cannon when he was killed in 1778, at the Battle of Monmouth, New Jersey?

9. Where did Commodore George Dewey fight a famous sea battle with the Spanish fleet?

10. Where is the tallest monument in the United States? It is on a battlefield and stands 567 feet high.

11. What two cities served as Confederate capitals during the Civil War?

12. Who was president of the Confederate States of America?

13. Who was the woman who lived in the White House when Washington, D.C., was attacked by the British during the War of 1812? She saved a noted painting of George Washington from possible destruction.

14. What group of pirates operating around Tripoli and Algiers in the Mediterranean Sea was an irritation to the United States government for a number of years?

15. How many United States citizens signed the Declaration of Independence?

16. What noted signer of the Declaration of Independence wrote large so that King George III would not need his glasses to read the signature?

17. What was the "Marine Turtle" which was invented by Richard Bushnell in 1776?

18. What was the importance of Jamestown in 1607?

19. What crop was grown commercially by the English for the first time at Jamestown, Virginia?

20. Who married Pocahontas?

21. What three events occurred in 1619, which changed life in Jamestown, Virginia?

22. What was the name of the first ship to sail around the world and prove that the earth was truly round?

23. What is the Bill of Rights?

24. What woman is given credit for making the first United States flag?

25. What was the most famous "party" given in Colonial America?

26. Who wrote Uncle Tom's Cabin, which had much to do with American thought in the North concerning slavery?

27. Who was the only United States President to be impeached?

28. What United States President spoke of a Square Deal?

29. What United States President had a New Deal?

30. What great poem was written as a result of a great naval bombardment at Fort McHenry at Baltimore, Maryland?

31. Who was the last Dutch governor of New Amsterdam before it was taken by the British and named New York? He had a wooden leg and a terrible temper.

32. What American President once fought and won a duel over his favorite race horse?

33. What was the name of the first transcontinental railroad? It was completed May 10, 1869, near Ogden, Utah.

34. What was the war in which Jefferson Davis and Abraham Lincoln fought together against the Indians?

35. What is the "big ditch"?

36. What two men have been three times nominated for the office of the President of the United States and have three times failed to be elected?

37. What famous organization of antislavery people helped escaped slaves by hiding and feeding them on their way to Canada?

38. Who was the schoolteacher the British hanged without a trial during the Revolution?

39. What noted newspaperman lost his wife, the presidency, and his life within one month?

40. What old woman, according to a poem by John Greenleaf Whittier, waved the "Stars and Stripes" at the Confederate invaders of Maryland under General "Stonewall" Jackson?

41. What is the name of America's oldest college still in operation, and when was it founded?

42. Who do we usually think of as leader of the Rough Riders?

43. What war saw the Battle of San Juan Hill?

44. Why did many Northerners learn to hate the name of Mrs. Mary Surratt?

45. What was the name of the Confederate raider which sank millions of dollars of Union shipping during the Civil War?

46. What islands did the United States buy from Denmark in 1917 for $25,000,000?

47. What Southern beauty acted as a spy for the Confederacy during the Civil War?

48. Who was the Southern spy who urged the Confederate troops to attack at Bull Run in 1861?

49. What inventor died at the Alamo, and what did he invent?

50. Who told John Alden to speak for himself?

51. What was the name of the famous clipper ship which sailed from New York to San Francisco around Cape Horn in eighty-nine days, eighteen hours?

52. Who was the newspaper publisher who in 1735 was tried for making harsh but true statements about the New York governor? This was the test of freedom of the press in America.

53. Who wrote the "Battle Hymn of the Republic"?

54. What famous trail was followed by the first transcontinental railroad?

55. Who was the pretty girl who carried messages from Benedict Arnold to John André concerning the betrayal of West Point?

56. Who founded the American Red Cross?

57. What American Negro educator was born a slave but went on to found the Tuskegee Institute in Alabama for the education of Negroes?

58. What great American naval hero became an admiral in the Russian Navy?

59. Who organized America's first city fire department at Philadelphia?

60. What famous ship did John Ericsson design for the United States?

61. Who was the man who left his deathbed and rode eighty miles through a blinding storm to sign the Declaration of Independence?

62. Who was the Vice-President of the United States who resigned because he didn't agree with the President's policies

toward the state of South Carolina, the Vice-President's home state?

63.   Where and when was Virginia Dare, the first white child born in the New World, born?

64.   What is the oldest city in the United States, and who settled it?

65.   Why did the South call the Union blockade of their ports "Lincoln's Great Snake"?

66.   What name do we know Jonathan Chapman by, and what did he do to earn the name?

67.   Why was the 1824 presidential election an unpopular election with many?

68.   What four wars did the United States enter in April?

69.   What noted President had no predecessor nor successor?

70.   What United States President once edited the *Marion Star* in an Ohio town?

71.   What land did we buy from a European dictator, and how much did we pay?

72.   Who led the Green Mountain Boys during the Revolution?

73.   How was Andrew Johnson different from all other governors of Tennessee?

74.   What great naval engagement ended with the Americans' total loss standing at eight men wounded as compared with the loss of ten ships by the enemy?

75.   What historic battle was fought after the war was over?

History in Error

It is not at all uncommon for people to be in error concerning history. Historians are often in error when they attempt to predict the future in light of the past. If you keep this in mind, surely the authors cannot be blamed for the fact that they have made a few errors concerning historical fact in the following paragraphs. To be quite exact, which is what all historians wish, we have allowed eighteen errors to creep into the following eighteen paragraphs. We would appreciate it if you would locate those errors for us and correct them. Each paragraph contains one error of fact. Should you spot all eighteen errors, you are on your way to becoming a recognized historian. Sixteen or seventeen corrections still tell us that you have a good knowledge of history. Ten is a passing score, but one really should detect at least fifteen errors in order to consider himself a good historian.

We have provided answers for you on page 224.

1. When the British left Boston and marched toward Lexington and Concord, they intended to capture and destroy materials assembled by the Colonists. They also wished to capture Sam Adams and John Hancock. Paul Revere rode to warn the citizens of the coming of the Redcoats. When he reached Concord, however, no one paid heed to his warning.

2. Many of the American nation's early explorers experienced Indian troubles. Often, the only way a leader could protect his followers was by convincing the Indians that he was a god. Of course, a god could not be killed nor die. For this reason when de Soto died, his men weighted his body and placed it in the Missouri River under cover of darkness, thus hoping to keep his death from being discovered by the Indians.

3. Early in World War II it became evident that Great Britain would surely perish unless she could be supplied across the Atlantic. German submarines and naval vessels made ocean shipping hazardous and uncertain. Losses ran into hundreds of ships and thousands of lives as the Battle of the Atlantic raged. The German ship *Bismarck* was an extremely powerful ship and one much feared by the Allies. When American planes finally sank this German vessel on May 27, 1941, shortly after it had sunk the British *Hood*, the people of England were much heartened by the news.

4. American history records many terrible air crashes, some resulting in deaths to as many as a hundred or more people. It is interesting to note that not all these crashes involved airplanes. Many involved dirigibles. One of the most famous of the great crashes involved the German zeppelin Hindenburg. It

burned while attempting a mooring at Lakehurst, New Jersey, May 6, 1937. It caused the loss of thirty-six lives, making it the worst air disaster to that date.

5. The Union victory at the Battle of Antietam on September 17, 1862, had several far-reaching effects. One was to keep England and France from recognizing the Confederacy. A second was to give Lincoln enough confidence in his forces to enable him to issue the Emancipation Proclamation. This historic document freed as of January 1, 1863, all slaves in the United States.

6. Because of his part in bringing about Aaron Burr's defeat in the New York election of April 25, 1804, Alexander Hamilton was involved in a duel with Burr. Hamilton supposedly said that Burr was "a dangerous man, and one who ought not to be trusted with the reins of government." Burr demanded an explanation. This demand led to their famous duel on July 11, 1804. In spite of the wide publicity the duel received, Hamilton was never brought to trial for killing Burr.

7. One of the most famous events in the history of the westward expansion of America was the Battle of the Little Big Horn on June 26, 1876. During this battle Chief Sitting Bull and his followers completely annihilated Colonel George A. Custer and his troop of 264 men.

8. When Lincoln sent Secretary of State William H. Seward to negotiate with the Russian minister to the United States, Baron Edoard de Stoeckl, for the purchase of Alaska, many opposed the purchase. When the purchase price of $7,200,000 was made public, the terms "Seward's Folly" and "Seward's Icebox" became part of the American vocabulary. Though people condemned Seward and the government at the time for the purchase, history has shown the acquisition to have been one of our nation's best buys.

9. America's airlines are known the world over for their comfort and dependability. Some American airlines have maintained excellent safety records. Some few commercial airlines have never had a fatality in their operational history. Seaboard Airline is one commercial transportation line which has never had a plane

crash, nor had a plane with engine failure. All this is true in spite of the fact that they began their operations early in the twentieth century.

10. During the Spanish-American War the historic Battle of Manila Bay stirred the hearts of Americans everywhere. The battles of El Caney and San Juan Hill became the topic of discussion for days and weeks. Perhaps Colonel Theodore Roosevelt and the Rough Riders riding through a hail of bullets to capture San Juan Hill gave the American people something of which to be proud as an American. Whatever the reason, the Battle of San Juan Hill is probably as well remembered a name as exists in the history of America.

11. Few, if any, Americans of school age or older will ever forget the historic landing of the Pilgrims on the New England coast in 1620. But how many people fail to realize that these people, who were the first Europeans to land in New England, had already made several major moves in their search for religious freedom? They had previously left Scrooby, England, and moved to Amsterdam, Holland. From there they had moved to Leyden, Holland. In all it was twelve years after their arrival at Amsterdam before they landed in North America.

12. No one who lived during the World War II era will ever forget the frightful experiences undergone by the British people during the great bombing raids in the Battle of Britain during the late summer and fall of 1940. However, many forget the terror of the V-I "buzz bomb" which appeared on June 12, 1944, and brought destruction and suffering again to the British people. Had the Allies not been successful in their European offensive, the long-suffering citizens of the British Isles would have eventually had to endure the effects of the supersonic V-2 rockets which were designed to operate at over 3,000 miles per hour.

13. When Franklin D. Roosevelt became the leader of the American people, it was a time which called for positive measures to relieve a suffering and confused nation. His New Deal was designed to do just that. As quickly as possible after becoming

President he pushed for enactment of bills creating such famous measures and organizations as RFC, CCC, AAA, TVA, NRA, WPA, NIRA, PWA, and other famous New Deal measures.

14. Andrew Jackson's national fame was based in part on his military exploits during the War of 1812. Not the least of these noted achievements was his success at the Battle of New Orleans on January 8, 1815. During this historic battle Jackson with about 4,500 men thoroughly defeated the force of about 5,300 British troops. Jackson's troops, which included Kentucky and Tennessee riflemen armed with long rifles, outshot the British regulars during the two attacks made by the British. Though the great battle lasted little more than half an hour, British losses in killed and wounded amounted to over 2,000 as compared to Jackson's losses of eight killed and thirteen wounded. This overwhelming display of American military might brought the war to a speedy close. The Treaty of Ghent ending the war was signed soon after.

15. Born in Clark, Missouri, on February 12, 1893, Omar Nelson Bradley was destined to become a positive influence in the course of military affairs of the United States. Among the positions he has held in his military career have been teacher of mathematics at West Point for four years, member of the War Department general staff, commander of the Second United States Corps in the Tunisian campaign, field aide to General Eisenhower, commander of the Twelfth Army in Europe, head of the VA, and permanent chairman of the Joint Chiefs of Staff. With these posts as a part of his career it is small wonder that "the General in Spurs" is, and has been, a well-known figure in American military history.

16. In 1856, Jefferson Davis, who was Secretary of War under Franklin Pierce, was responsible for bringing to this country a number of camels to be used on a trial basis by the army in the deserts of the American Southwest. With the camels came three dozen camel drivers to aid the soldiers in the use of the camels. After an unsuccessful trial period it became apparent that the camels were not going to work well in

the United States Army. The camels were turned loose, and the camel drivers were all sent home. The interesting part of the entire affair is that for years travelers of the Texas and Arizona deserts would report in disbelief that they had seen a camel, or a herd of camels, on the desert. Perhaps even today the descendants of these original camels may yet roam the American southwestern deserts.

17. For the remaining members of the Confederate Army April 9, 1865, spelled the end of a long, hard military campaign. On that day General Robert E. Lee and General Ulysses S. Grant met at Appomattox Courthouse to agree on the terms of Lee's surrender. The terms agreed on by these generals were considered liberal by all concerned. Lee's soldiers were sent home without punishment. Confederate officers could keep their side arms. All war equipment was to be surrendered by the Southerners, but they were all allowed to keep privately owned horses and mules. This last meant much to General Lee as he would not have to part with his beloved horse Cincinnatus.

18. Of the many epic events and feats of endurance recorded in American history, none excel the story of Robert E. Peary and his quest for the South Pole despite tremendous odds. After several scientific voyages he attempted to reach the Pole during his 1905–06 voyage on the ship *Roosevelt*. He managed to struggle against the odds of weather and terrain to within 174 miles of the Pole before turning back. Again in 1908, he sailed on the *Roosevelt*. Better prepared to reach the Pole and more determined than ever, Peary, his Negro servant Matthew Henson, four Eskimos, and forty dogs reached the Pole on April 6, 1909. The ironic ending to the story came when another explorer claimed to have reached the Pole the previous year. Though scientists agreed with Peary, the other claim detracted from the honor which he felt was rightfully his.

Geographical Quizzes

Hidden States

It should be a simple matter for you to uncover the state names disguised in the following sentences. Since there are only fifty states from which to choose, don't expect much in the way of help from our clues.

1. Will you have Sal ask about the price of eggs when she is at the store?
(It wasn't a state in 1865.)
2. We have to do our week's washing tonight after work.
(It's west of the Mississippi.)
3. Here is that pie tin Diana wanted.
(Indians once lived in this state.)
4. Didn't that test exasperate you?
(It is larger than Wyoming and smaller than Alaska.)
5. Is a llama inexpensive to buy for a zoo?
(This state borders Canada.)
6. We are going to miss our industrious workers when they go on vacation.
(An American President came from this state not so long ago.)
7. When the drowning swimmer was rescued, he was more gone than alive.
(This state has a salt water border.)

8. As we listened, the sailor said, "Ahoy there, mates," as he greeted his friends.

(Here's another state which borders Canada.)

9. Would it be best to color a dog brown or black?

(In this state mountains are found.)

10. Will you have Ken tuck your blankets in tonight when he goes to bed?

(In our early history this state was in the "West.")

11. When you visited Ohio, was the weather hot?

(Yes, we know Ohio is there, but you need to find another state.)

12. Isn't the newly built Tampa Lab amazing!

(This state is found in the southern United States.)

13. There is a cut ahead in next year's budget I'm afraid.

(The hidden state is a rather large western state.)

14. Even Eva darns socks, so why don't you?

(Mining helped this land to become a state.)

15. Were the people in the citadel aware that the attack was soon to come?

(The Atlantic Ocean touches this state.)

16. When we were in Vermont, an airplane crashed.

(Look about two thousand miles from Vermont for our hidden state.)

17. Sever months into days and days into hours, and study each minute of each.

(Our bit of advice conceals the name of a New England state.)

18. Did you go to the airport to see Mary land?

(The needed answer names one of the original thirteen colonies.)

19. The florid and stylish writing of early authors is no longer popular.

(This state is popular, however, especially with tourists.)

20. Smilingly, he said, "O, hi, Omar. How are you?"

(You hardly need a clue to locate the name of the disguised midwestern state.)

Oh yes, on the above disguises you should have found at least fifteen if you've lived in the United States for more than a year. Sixteen through nineteen would not be bad scores for people who have had a class in geography within the last eighty years or so, and a score of twenty probably indicates that you peeked at the answers.

For those who declare the task impossible, a glance at page 226. should help.

The Naming of the States

Do you know the origin of the name of the state in which you live? Have you any idea how the other forty-nine state names came to be? After you have completed the following quiz, chances are you will be better informed concerning state name beginnings.

As is often the case in any study of name origins, there may be those who disagree with the facts presented here. In the states chosen to become a part of this quiz there seems to be little question but that the clues given correspond to those facts considered correct by historians.

After you have struggled with these twenty names, it might prove interesting to check on the names of the other thirty. They are just as interesting in their beginnings as are these.

1. What state's name comes from a Spanish word meaning "red"?

2. What state was named for an old French province?

3. Which state was named for the wife of Charles I, Queen Henrietta Maria?

4. Which state was named for a President of the United States?

5. Which state's name is a Russian version of an Eskimo word?

6. Which state's name means "mountainous" in Latin?

7. What state's name means "snow-clad" in Spanish?

8. Which state name means "green mountains" in French?

171

9. What western state was named for the site of an Indian massacre in Pennsylvania?

10. Which state got its name because Indians lived there?

11. Which state got its name from Lord De La Warr, the first governor of the Virginia Company?

12. Which state did Ponce de Leon name?

13. James Oglethorpe named what state after an English king?

14. Which state got its name from an English duke?

15. The name of what state includes the name of its founder and a word meaning "woodland"?

16. Which state's name in the Sioux tongue meant "south wind people"?

17. This state's name means "large river" in the Chippewa language.

18. The Chippewa's called this state "grassy place."

19. In Sioux language this state's name means "one who puts to sleep."

20. This state's name means "red man" in the Choctaw language.

A glance at the following rating scale might be in order after you check yourself on page 226.

Less than ten correct   —You weren't trying
Eleven to fifteen   —Not bad (for an elementary student, that is)
Sixteen to nineteen   —A bit of mild boasting might be in order
Twenty   —Wow!

Now for Nicknames

States, like people, are often nicknamed. Each of the states of the U.S. has a nickname; several have two. Nicknames usually describe an attribute of the state, something commonly found within the state, a reference to the state's history, or advertise the state in chamber-of-commerce fashion.

The following quiz gives a clue as to the nickname of each of the fifty states. All you need to do is to identify the nickname and decide to which state it belongs. Sounds easy, but watch out!

State nicknames are fun to identify by oneself, but they also are the basis for group contests. A leader may call for states to match the nicknames he gives, or for nicknames to match the states he names. The game may prove more interesting if each player in turn calls for the nickname of a given state. A little imagination will enable you to use these nicknames in a variety of games and quizzes.

When you are at a loss for an answer, look for help on page 226.

Each of the following questions begins—What state nickname:
1.   Indicates this state gives one the chance to get ahead?
2.   Indicates an unwillingness to accept things without proof?
3.   Reflects the fact that its flag contains but one star?
4.   Names a fur-bearing animal which was much sought by trappers of the Old West?
5.   Names a quarried building stone?
6.   Gives an indication of the small size of this state?
7.   Tells the world this state gave women the right to vote before other states followed suit?
8.   Names a beautiful flowering tree found in the South?
9.   Comes from the name of a natural wonder found within the state?
10.   Is a word signifying affection and kindness?
11.   Names a grass?
12.   Gives the name of a savage and much feared animal of the North?
13.   Indicates this state is enthralling?
14.   Tells us much of the state is hilly and mountainous?
15.   Reminds one of something valuable which has been hidden?

16. Gives the name of a large tree seed often carried for good luck?

17. Is the name of a plant related to the palms?

18. Names the stone at the top of an arch which enables the arch to stand?

19. Names the home of an industrious insect?

20. Leads one to believe that much of the state is relatively flat?

21. Gives the name of a large beaked, fish-eating bird?

22. Might indicate keenness of sight?

23. Makes historical reference to the use of one of its products by the Royal Navy?

24. Gives the location of the state? Its second nickname tells of one of its chief products.

25. Tells of a solar phenomenon common to this state?

26. Makes reference to the age of the state? Another nickname calls to mind an early settlement.

27. Names a small rodent? A second nickname makes reference to a heavenly body.

28. Might well be a chamber-of-commerce advertisement?

29. Gives the name of an animal which despite its small size is a noted fighter when angered?

30. Refers to the illegal arrivals in a noted land rush?

31. Mentions an animal of the dry lands? Its second nickname tells of the sun.

32. Should bring to mind the efforts of members of this state in the American nation's wars?

33. Describes a farming activity?

34. Lets us know of its status as an old and well organized state in our history?

35. Is the common term describing any precious stone?

36. Tells one and all that it joined the Union one hundred years after the Union was formed?

37. Mentions the fact that this state first ratified the Constitution? Its second nickname is that of a stone prized by women the world over.

38. Names a yellow flower?

39. Mentions a precious metal once mined in abundance within the state?

40. Indicates a lush area in terms of food?

41. Would lead one to believe the state to be heavily forested with conifers?

42. Names an Indian tribe? Another nickname brings the name of a bird to mind.

43. Tells the name of a native of the Pine Barrens in this state? It might also create an image of a part of the body made sticky by a black, gummy substance.

44. Indicates an extremely valuable state?

45. Tells of a southern state with vast potential?

46. Lays claim to being the first state to have a written plan of government?

47. Mentions its part in fostering freedom? Another nickname might bring to mind the Mason-Dixon Line.

48. Indicates the presence of vegetation-covered mountains?

49. Tells that this state is dominating in concept?

50. Appeared in the title of a book concerning a teacher in this state?

In and Around America's Great Cities

Who hasn't taken a sight-seeing tour at one time or another? We have prepared an imaginary sight-seeing tour for you to take with us. For each city we visit we will take you to four interesting, scenic, or historic places located in and around the city. After you have seen these four places, tell what city you have visited.

The tour works well as a group game. A leader might give the four sights visited to the players who list the cities as they "tour" them. The player with the most correctly identified cities wins. Another possibility is to give one point of interest at a time, until a player correctly names the city. The first correct answer wins the point. Yet another way to conduct the "tour" is to name the sights seen slowly enough so that players may write the name of the sight which enabled them to identify the city. Give five points if they get the city on the first sight, three for the second, two for the third, and only one point if they don't identify the city until hearing the final clue. The player with the highest score is declared winner. Why not consider the ten cities here as merely a beginning, and on your own set up some interesting tours to give the group? Happy sight-seeing!

Page 228 will help if you get lost.

1. In or near what American city are found:
   A. Fitzsimons, the largest military hospital in the nation
   B. A good-domed capitol building
   C. Red Rocks Amphitheater
   D. A U.S. mint

2. Where would you see:
   A. Fisherman's Wharf
   B. Trolleys
   C. Chinatown
   D. Golden Gate Bridge

3. In what city are located:
   A. Grant's Tomb
   B. Kennedy Airport
   C. The Fulton Street Fish Market
   D. The United Nations buildings

4. Where might you find:
   A. Tulane University
   B. Isaac Delgado Museum of Art
   C. The French Quarter
   D. The Mardi Gras festival

5. In which American city are located:
   A. Marshall Field department store
   B. Great rail yards
   C. Huge stock yards
   D. The Loop

6. Where would you see:
   A. Beacon Hill
   B. Old North Church
   C. Back Bay
   D. The Liberty Tree
7. In what city would you be if you saw:
   A. A U.S. mint
   B. Franklin Institute
   C. Betsy Ross House
   D. Independence Hall
8. Where are you when you observe:
   A. Griffith Park
   B. The University of Southern California
   C. The corner of Hollywood and Vine
   D. MGM, Twentieth Century-Fox, and other such studios
9. What city is the home of:
   A. The Library of Congress
   B. Blair House
   C. The Lincoln Memorial
   D. The White House
10. Where would you see:
    A. The Virginia Museum of Fine Arts
    B. John Marshall's house
    C. St. John's Church
    D. The White House of the Confederacy

Where in the World?

In the United States we have hundreds of places known to all. We use these place names in our everyday conversation with little thought as to their location. We challenge you to give the state in which each of the following points of interest is located.

A perfect score is to be expected, but may be hard to attain. One or two errors is not bad, but more than five errors might well indicate that a session with a geography book wouldn't hurt.

No matter how sure you are that your answers are correct, better check with page 228 just to be certain.

1. The Alamo
2. Donner Pass
3. West Point
4. Annapolis
5. Pike's Peak
6. The Ozarks
7. Carlsbad Caverns
8. The Superstition Mountains
9. Grand Canyon
10. Gettysburg
11. Bunker Hill
12. Mount Rushmore National Memorial
13. Mount McKinley
14. Diamond Head
15. Mesa Verde
16. The Green Mountains
17. Okefenokee Swamp
18. The Great Salt Lake
19. Golden Gate Bridge
20. Alcatraz
21. Death Valley
22. Crater Lake National Park
23. Mount Rainier
24. Old Faithful
25. Grand Tetons National Park
26. King Ranch
27. The Bad Lands
28. Monticello
29. Cape Cod
30. Fisherman's Wharf
31. Greenwich Village
32. Fort Knox

A Capital Scramble

Here is a quickie to make sure you haven't forgotten your states and capitals. We've given you ten state capitals. All you have to do to complete the puzzle is to supply the state name which matches the given capital. When you have completed your list of ten state names, take the beginning letter from the name of each state and use those ten letters to form a word.

It might help you to know that the word you are attempting to form is the last name of one of the Revolutionary War heroes. A major American city also bears the same name.

Capital	State
Montgomery	1. _____
Olympia	2. _____

Honolulu	3. _____
Columbia	4. _____
Atlanta	5. _____
Indianapolis	6. _____
Carson City	7. _____
Santa Fé	8. _____
Columbus	9. _____
Nashville	10. _____

In case you got stuck, page 228 tells how to unscramble the letters correctly.

States and Capitals Criss-Cross

Here is another criss-cross which should help you review your capital cities while having a little fun. Again, let us suggest that you either paper clip a transparent sheet of paper over the page upon which to write or that you use a sheet of squared paper and build your criss-cross as you go. Don't worry about drawing in our squares. As your puzzle grows, it will take care of itself.

The only acceptable score is a perfect one; otherwise, your puzzle will not fit together. Page 228 will aid you should you need help, but you really shouldn't require a great deal of help with this one.

We have given the capitals of our fifty states below. You supply the state name, and place it in the correct place in the puzzle.

Capitals

Across		Down	
2.	Raleigh	1.	Baton Rouge
4.	Jackson	3.	Lansing
5.	Frankfort	6.	Carson City
7.	Charleston	8.	Atlanta
10.	Pierre	9.	Concord
11.	Montpelier	10.	Columbia

179

(Across cont.)

14. Honolulu
17. Salem
18. Juneau

(Down cont.)

12. Augusta
13. Nashville
15. Montgomery

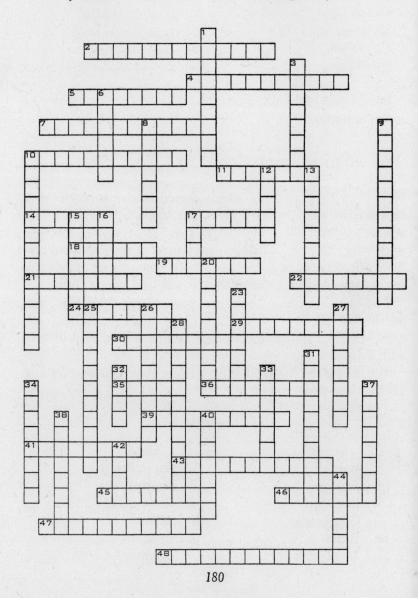

(Across cont.)		(Down cont.)	
19.	Cheyenne	16.	Boise
21.	Oklahoma City	17.	Columbus
22.	Dover	20.	St. Paul
24.	Phoenix	23.	Albany
29.	Madison	25.	Providence
30.	Trenton	26.	Santa Fé
35.	Austin	27.	Jefferson City
36.	Little Rock	28.	Harrisburg
39.	Sacramento	31.	Olympia
41.	Springfield	32.	Salt Lake City
43.	Bismarck	33.	Indianapolis
45.	Annapolis	34.	Richmond
46.	Helena	37.	Lincoln
47.	Hartford	38.	Denver
48.	Boston	40.	Tallahassee
		42.	Des Moines
		44.	Topeka

Coast to Coast and Border to Border

It is interesting to note that about two-thirds of the states in the American nation are boundary states; they either border another country or have an ocean coast. Before you run to an atlas to check this, why not take the following quiz? Its results may be a revelation to you.

By rights no one should miss any of the points on the quiz, but we'll bet that those getting a perfect score are few and far between. After you have tested yourself, you will enjoy giving a couple of the rougher questions to your friends.

1. Chances are that not one person in five can name the thirteen states which border Canada in the order in which they appear on a map. Can you? Don't forget the two states whose only boundary between them and Canada is a Great Lake, but do not include Wisconsin which, because of Michigan's Isle Royale, is not considered to border Canada.

2. An easier task is to list the four states bordering Mexico.

3. Another fairly simple job is to name the five states which touch the Gulf of Mexico.

4. Naming the states touching the Pacific Ocean shouldn't be too difficult either.

5. In conclusion, why not list the states which border the Atlantic Ocean. Don't forget those states with saltwater bays.

If you haven't peeked already, turn to page 229.

Next Door Neighbors

Can you name the states which border the state where you live? Can you list the names of the states bordering each of them? Here is a chance to check your knowledge of place geography in an interesting fashion. This two-part quiz requires only that you know or figure out which states border the states given. Every time a blank appears, it is to be filled with a state name. The names and blanks given show approximately where the states are in relation to one another. It wouldn't be fair to use a map or globe when taking this quiz.

The first part of the quiz has a possible high score of fifty-eight. Any less than forty is failing, below forty-eight is just passing, below fifty-two is average, below fifty-five is above average, fifty-five to fifty-seven is very good, and a perfect score is just that—perfect.

For the second part you need to score all eleven points to have a really acceptable score; but since everyone is entitled to one mistake, a score of ten correct will be considered passing.

If you don't want to check yourself with an atlas, turn to page 230 for the correct answers.

Part I

1 _____

6 _____

2 _____

Wyoming

3 _____

5 _____   4 _____

1 _____

4 _____

Alabama 2 _____

3 _____

1 _____ 2 _____

5 _____ Nevada 3 _____

4 _____

1 _____

2 _____

8 _____ Tennessee 3 _____

7 _____

6 _____ 4 _____

5 _____

1 _____

6 _____ Pennsylvania 2 _____

3 _____

5 _____ 4 _____

1 _____

6 _____ 2 _____

5 _____ Oklahoma

3 _____

4 _____

1 _____

5 _____ West Virginia 2 _____

4 _____

3 _____

183

4 _____

1 _____

Wisconsin

3 _____

2 _____

_____

1 _____

2 _____

5 _____ Massachusetts

4 _____

3 _____

_____

1 _____

8 _____

2 _____

Missouri

7 _____

3 _____

6 _____

5 _____   4 _____

Part II

All you need to do now is to fill in the one missing state as indicated by the blank.

1 _____ Idaho

Oregon

New Hampshire   2 _____

Alabama   Georgia

3 _____

4 _____

Vermont
Massachusetts
Connecticut
New Jersey

Pennsylvania

Virginia

Tennessee   5

Georgia   South Carolina

Arkansas

Mississippi

Texas

6 _____

Utah

Nevada

7 _____

Colorado

California

New Mexico

Michigan

Illinois   8 _____   Ohio

Kentucky

10 _____

(No bordering states)

Montana 9 _____ Minnesota

South Dakota

11 _____

(No bordering states)

Points of the Compass

Here is a little quiz which will test your sense of direction concerning places found within the United States. Each statement contains one or more directional clues to the location of the missing city or point of interest. Try to "find" the described place without the help of a map, but using a map is not against the rules.

You will want to check your answers against ours, which are found on page 231. Then you will probably want to make up a set of your own questions to give to others.

If you are interested in a score, assume that less than eighteen correct means you don't know your directions. Over eighteen but less than twenty-four places you in the ranks of the average American. A higher score tells you that you are well educated along these lines.

1. What state capital is found one hundred miles north of Denver?

2. Do you know the name of a renowned lake located northwest of Provo and south of Pocatello?

3. North of Anchorage and southwest of Fairbanks is a 20,000 foot mountain. What is its name?

4. Which great port is found east of San Antonio and north of Galveston?

5. Can you name the lake which is east of Milwaukee and west of Grand Rapids?

6. What is the name of the cape east of Raleigh which has been the scene of many ship wrecks?

7. What river city is northeast of Wichita and west of St. Louis?

8. Are you able to name the coast city located south of Palm Beach and southeast of Tampa?

9. What national park is northeast of Boise and south of Helena?

10. A city noted for its flour mills is southwest of Rochester and south of Niagara Falls. What is its name?

11. What capital city is found west of Dayton and south of South Bend?

12. Which great stockyard city is southwest of Des Moines and south of Sioux City?

13. Can you identify the coastal city located north of Tijuana and southeast of Los Angeles?

14. A city founded early in our history and now a state capital is located north of Albuquerque and west of Amarillo. What city is this?

15. Can you name a southern rail center found southeast of Chattanooga and east of Birmingham?

16. What is the coastal capital city found southeast of Waipahu and southwest of Kaneohe?

17. What scenic wonder is north of Flagstaff and east of Las Vegas?

18. Do you know the name of the manufacturing city found northwest of Cleveland and north of Toledo?

19. Which capital city is west of Meridian and east of Vicksburg?

20. Are you able to identify the river city west of St. Paul and southwest of Duluth?

21 What major city is located east of Fort Worth and northwest of Houston?

22. The home of a noted educational institution is found south of Baltimore and east of Washington, D.C. What city is this?

23. A city noted for rail yards and its meat packing industry is found northwest of Gary and south of Racine. What is its name?

24. Can you name the lake located west of Montpelier and northeast of Syracuse?

25. Which state capital is north of Pierre and west of Fargo?

It's a Big Country

No one who has crossed the United States by auto, bus, or train can help realizing that it's a huge country. We have supplied some straight-line distances from several points in the nation and offer two choices as to your location were you the given distance from the city named.

This can be fun as a group game or contest, in which case our twenty examples will serve as only starters when the group begins coming up with distances on their own. One thing is certain, whether this quiz is used by one or by a group, it will develop an awareness of the size of the U.S.

1. If you were 525 miles south of Salt Lake City, Utah, would you be near Phoenix, Arizona, or the Grand Canyon?

2. Which is 800 miles west of Denver, Colorado—Las Vegas, Nevada, or Reno, Nevada.

3. Is Portland, Oregon, or Seattle, Washington, nearly 600 miles north of San Francisco, California?

4. Is Des Moines, Iowa, or Kansas City, Missouri, nearly 850 miles north of Houston, Texas?

5. Would you be in Indianapolis, Indiana, or Chicago, Illinois, if you were 625 miles northwest of Atlanta, Georgia?

6. Is Jackson, Mississippi, or Mobile, Alabama, 250 miles west of Montgomery, Alabama?

7. If you were 675 miles north of El Paso, Texas, would you be more apt to be in Colorado Springs, Colorado, or Cheyenne, Wyoming?

8. Is Boise, Idaho, or Helena, Montana, found 800 miles north of San Diego, California?

9. Would you expect to find Little Rock, Arkansas, or Jefferson City, Missouri, 750 miles south of St. Paul, Minnesota?

10. When you are 500 miles north of Nashville, Tennessee, are you near Duluth, Minnesota, or Grand Rapids, Michigan?

11. Is Columbia, South Carolina, or Richmond, Virginia, to be found 600 miles north of Miami, Florida?

12. Is Philadelphia, Pennsylvania, or Boston, Massachusetts, found 1,150 miles east of Lincoln, Nebraska?

13. If you traveled 400 miles north of Memphis, Tennessee, would you be in Peoria, Illinois, or Chicago, Illinois?

14. Were you to leave New Orleans, Louisiana, and travel 1,000 miles northeast, would you stop in Washington, D.C., or New York, New York?

15. Is Wichita, Kansas, or Omaha, Nebraska, closer to being 375 miles north of Tulsa, Oklahoma?

16. Would you be in Washington, D.C., or Wheeling, West Virginia, if you were 700 miles east of Springfield, Illinois?

17. Is Atlanta, Georgia, or Montgomery, Alabama, about 450 miles south of Columbus, Ohio?

18. Would a trip of 450 miles west of Raleigh, North Carolina, take you to Nashville, Tennessee, or Memphis, Tennessee?

19. When you travel 175 miles southwest from Buffalo, New York, are you in Columbus, Ohio, or Cleveland, Ohio?

20. Is St. Louis, Missouri, or Des Moines, Iowa, located about 1,100 miles northwest of Miami, Florida?

If there are any doubts about correct answers, better check with page 231. Over ten errors tell us that you haven't paid the gas bill for the family auto on any of the trips mentioned. Less than five errors suggest the possibility that you have traveled quite a bit, and a perfect score might indicate that you are a map maker by trade.

Why not try our next quiz "Faraway Places," which takes us on twenty auto trips between United States cities?

Faraway Places

These quiz questions deal with auto traveling distances between pairs of cities in the United States. Following the names of the cities, are two approximate distances. One of these figures is close to the exact mileage between the two cities if one were to travel by auto.

This set of cities might well serve as the starting point for a game of your own devising. Such a game or quiz is fun for those who have traveled or who wish to travel.

A score of less than fifteen correct indicates a poor sense of distance, while only two errors or less show more than a little knowledge concerning the size of our nation. If you score between sixteen and eighteen, you've done well.

You travel from:	Your auto mileage is:
1. New York, New York, to San Francisco, California	3,050 or 3,450 miles
2. Cleveland, Ohio, to Baltimore, Maryland	350 or 550 miles
3. Pittsburgh, Pennsylvania, to St. Louis, Missouri	450 or 600 miles
4. Salt Lake City, Utah, to Dallas, Texas	1,500 or 1,250 miles
5. Chicago, Illinois, to Cheyenne, Wyoming	1,000 or 1,200 miles
6. Denver, Colorado, to Los Angeles, California	1,200 or 1,400 miles

7. Kansas City, Missouri, to
   St. Louis, Missouri   250 or 350 miles
8. Milwaukee, Wisconsin,
   to Portland, Oregon   2,100 or 1,500 miles
9. Washington, D.C., to
   Providence, Rhode Island   600 or 400 miles
10. Albany, New York, to
    New York, New York   170 or 225 miles
11. Portland, Maine, to Cin-
    cinnati, Ohio   1,150 or 950 miles
12. Cleveland, Ohio, to Mi-
    ami, Florida   1,300 or 1,500 miles
13. New Orleans, Louisiana,
    to Washington, D.C.   1,500 or 1,225 miles
14. Atlanta, Georgia, to Sa-
    vannah, Georgia   250 or 150 miles
15. Dallas, Texas, to Denver,
    Colorado   800 or 600 miles
16. San Antonio, Texas, to
    Chicago, Illinois   975 or 1,275 miles
17. Philadelphia, Pennsylva-
    nia, to Portland, Maine   400 or 600 miles
18. Boston, Massachusetts, to
    Detroit, Michigan   1,000 or 750 miles
    (Stay inside U.S.)
19. Washington, D.C., to
    Charleston, West Vir-
    ginia   350 or 550 miles
20. Memphis, Tennessee, to
    Helena, Montana   2,200 or 1,800 miles

To see just how far away some places really are, turn to page
231.

America, a Land of Great Rivers

Without the use of rivers as avenues of transportation the settlement of the interior of the United States would have been

delayed greatly. Without the rivers, poets, songwriters, and novelists would be hard pressed for content in many instances. Anything which has proved to be so much a part of American life should be known to all Americans, but is this really the case? Try the following quiz and see whether you know the rivers of America. If you can identify all of them correctly, you have an exceptional knowledge of our country. If you only miss one or two, you must have paid good attention in your classes on American geography. Three or four wrong is just passing, but five or more errors can't really be considered as a satisfactory grade on this quiz.

The line refers to the length of the river. Dots along the length of the line give approximate location of points listed above and below the river line. Beneath each river line are found two bits of historical, geographical, or general information which should give you additional clues to the identity of the river in question.

To check your answers, page 232 should set you straight.

1

Lake County, Colorado

•————————————————•————————————•

                                Tulsa   Mississippi River

A. The first structure erected by Americans in Colorado was a fort built along this river by Captain Zebulon Pike and his party in 1806.

B. This river flows through the capital city of Arkansas.

2

Henderson Lake, Essex County,
    New York

•————————————————————•————————————•

                           Albany   New York City

A. The Erie Canal in 1825 linked this river with Lake Erie and the capital of New York state, Albany.

B. This river was named for an English explorer who, when sailing under the Dutch flag, discovered the river and claimed the area for Holland in 1609.

3

Madison County, Montana   Kansas City

•————————•————————•————————•

            Omaha   St. Louis, Missouri

A. This river forms a part of America's longest river system.

B. The vast area drained by this river was part of the Louisiana Purchase in 1803.

4

Lake Itasca, Minnesota   Memphis

•————————•————————•————————•

         St. Louis   New Orleans, Louisiana

A. This river is often referred to as the "Father of Waters."

B. America's most famous river pilot, Mark Twain, immortalized this river and the lives of the people along it.

5

San Juan County,
      Colorado   El Paso

•————————•————————•————————•

      Albuquerque   Brownsville, Texas

A. The boundary between Mexico and Texas is formed by this river.

B. Many illegal immigrants entered the United States by swimming or wading across this river—hence the term "wetbacks."

6

Rocky Mountain National
     Park, Colorado   Mexico

•————————•————————•————————•

      Grand Canyon   Gulf of California

A. Hoover Dam, located on this river, provides electric power for millions of people.

B. In Spanish, the name of this river means "red."

7

Columbia Lake,
    British Columbia   Bonneville Dam

•————————•————————•————————•

    Grand Coulee Dam   Astoria

A.   This river was named after Captain Robert Gray's flagship in 1792.

B.   Lewis and Clark followed this river to the Pacific Ocean in 1805.

8

Hancock, New York

•————————————————•————————————————•

                              Philadelphia   Delaware Bay

A.   General Washington crossed this river on Christmas Eve of 1776 to surprise the Hessian soldiers in Trenton, New Jersey.

B.   The eastern border of Pennsylvania between New York and New Jersey is formed by this river.

9

Botetourt County,
    Virginia   Richmond

•————————•————————————•————————————•

         Lynchburg   Hampton Roads

A.   The *Monitor* and *Merrimac* fought at the mouth of this river.

B.   The first permanent English settlement in the New World was established on this river.

10

Mora County, New Mexico

•————————————————•————————————•

                              Carlsbad   Rio Grande

A.   _____ Bill was a popular tall tale of the nineteenth century.

B.   This river is one of the main tributaries of the Rio Grande.

11

Leflore County,
    Mississippi   Belzoni

•————•————————————•————————————•

    Greenwood   Mississippi River

A.   The name of this river is an Indian word meaning "River of Death."

B.   When the water is low, the hulk of a Union gunboat sunk during the Civil War is visible in this river.

193

12

Otsego Lake   Wilkes Barre

•————————•————————•————————•

       Binghampton, New York   Chesapeake Bay

A. The capital of Pennsylvania is located on this river.

B. This is the most northern major river emptying into Chesapeake Bay.

13

Charlton County,
    Georgia   Demory Hill

•————————•————————————•——•

       White Springs   Gulf of Mexico

A. The river rises in the Okefenokee Swamp.

B. Stephen Collins Foster immortalized this river in his ballad "Old Folks at Home."

14

Mountains of northern
    Virginia

•————————•————————————————•

       Fredericksburg   Chesapeake Bay

A. This river played a vital role in the movements of the Army of Northern Virginia and the Army of the Potomac during the Civil War.

B. In October of 1863, Union forces handed General Lee a stinging defeat on the banks of this river.

15

Lincoln County, Nebraska

•————————————————————————•

       Kearney   Missouri River

A. The north and south branches of this river coming from Wyoming and Colorado were favorite routes into the fur country of the Rocky Mountains.

B. Today's extensive use of water for irrigation leaves the river almost dry much of the year.

16

Darke County, Ohio   Terre Haute

•————•————————————•————————•

       LaFayette   Ohio River

A.   The river forms the border between southern Illinois and southern Indiana.

B.   George Rogers Clark seized Vincennes on the banks of this river in 1778.

17

Pittsburgh   Cincinnati

•———•——•————————•————————————•

Wheeling   Louisville   Mississippi River

A.   At the confluence of the Allegheny and Monongahela rivers this river begins. In 1754, the French built Fort Duquesne which later became the English Fort Pitt and eventually the American city of Pittsburgh.

B.   This river forms the boundary between Indiana and Kentucky.

18

Hampshire County,
   West Virginia   Washington, D.C.

•————————•————————•————————•

Harper's Ferry   Chesapeake Bay

A.   This river forms the boundary between Virginia and Maryland.

B.   It is closely associated with the life of America's first President.

19

Teton County, Wyoming

•——•————•————————————•

Idaho Falls   Pocatello   Columbia, Washington

A.   Along this river may be seen the famous Thousand Springs which flow beneath a lava plateau to empty into the river.

B.   This river formed famous Hell's Canyon.

20

Yukon Territory,
   Canada   Holy Cross

•————————•————————•————————•

Dawson   Bering Sea

A.   It is the fifth largest river in North America.

B.   This river passes through the famous Klondike gold field.

195

States and Their River Namesakes

It probably comes as no surprise to most people that the United States has many rivers bearing the names of states, or vice-versa. This puzzler asks that you supply the names of the states through which or along the border of which these state-named rivers flow. Some of these rivers are fairly small and are confined to only one state. Others, like the mighty Mississippi, can be viewed from twenty percent of our states.

When you've done your best, check yourself on page 232 and be prepared to be surprised in several cases.

If you can provide correct answers for fifty or more of the needed states, chances are you are too smart for us; but if you supply less than thirty correct states, it is possible that we were too smart for you. A perfect score, by the way, would lead us to believe that you either have your doctorate in United States geography or are very lucky, if not both.

1. Colorado River—two rivers found in six states
2. Alabama River—located in one state
3. Arkansas River—four states are required here
4. Connecticut River—you need four more states
5. Delaware River—you'll have to come up with five states for these two rivers
6. Illinois River—there are three rivers by this name in four states
7. Iowa River—found in only one state
8. Kansas River—found in only one state
9. Kentucky River—again, only one state needed
10. Minnesota River—still only found in one state
11. Mississippi River—better come up with ten states for this one
12. Missouri River—seven states will do here
13. Ohio River—six more states will see you through
14. Tennessee River—only four states necessary this time
15. Wisconsin River—an easy one to end on for only one state is needed to answer

The Colorful United States

Few will deny that the United States is a colorful country. This quiz should show the emphasis placed on color by the founders of the American nation. Use the quiz for self testing, for group quizzing, or for rotational group questioning. When you have done your best, check yourself on page 232.

Try to supply the state or states in which the following "colored" geographical features are to be found. The number following the name of the feature indicates the number of states you need to supply. If you wish to keep score, give one point for each correct answer and deduct two for each error.

1. Black Bayou (1)
2. Black Canyon (1)
3. Black Hills (1)
4. Black Mesa (2)
5. Black Mountains (1)
6. Blue Bayou (1)
7. Blue Mesa (1)
8. Blue Mountains (4)
9. Brown Cliffs (1)
10. Green Bay (2)
11. Green Mountains (2)
12. Green Swamp (1)
13. Orange Cliffs (1)
14. Pink Cliffs (1)
15. Red Creek (1)
16. Silver Creek (3)
17. White Mountains (1)
18. Yellow Cliff (1)
19. Yellow Creek (1)

A score of over twenty-five is too good to be true, over twenty is excellent, between ten and twenty is good, and less than ten is very poor.

Colored Rivers

Long before Hollywood was using color on the screen, we were using colors to name our rivers. The following color selections should provide food for thought for several minutes or more (probably much more). In most cases several rivers of the same name are involved, though not always. This one takes some thought and will prove a bit difficult for all but the dedicated students of geography or the seasoned travelers.

A score of forty or more correct out of the possible forty-seven is very good. Twenty or more right isn't too bad, but a score of less than twenty is not commendable.

1. Twelve states play host to a Black River. What are they?

2. You can find a Blue River in three states. Can you name those states?

3. What is the only state to have a Brown River?

4. Green Rivers flow in seven states. How many can you identify correctly?

5. In seven states may be found a Red River. We'll bet you can't name all seven.

6. White Rivers are to be found in thirteen of our states. Do you know the states?

7. You doubtless know that the Yellow River is native to China, but can you name four states through which rivers by the same name flow?

Now, turn to page 233 for the answers.

Answers

Answers to Quizzes from History

Discovering the New World

$$\overline{\underset{1}{E}\ \underset{2}{X}\ \underset{3}{P}\ \underset{4}{L}\ \underset{5}{O}\ \underset{6}{R}\ \underset{7}{A}\ \underset{8}{T}\ \underset{9}{I}\ \underset{10}{O}\ \underset{11}{N}}$$

Exploration Criss-Cross

Across	Down
1. Leif Ericson	2. Columbus
4. Cabrillo	3. Priest
5. Cartier	4. Champlain
7. Pinta	6. Isabella
9. Gilbert	8. Niña
12. Santa Maria	10. Virginia Dare
15. Roanoke	11. John Smith
16. Hispaniola	13. Map
18. Spice	14. Verrazano
19. Cabeza de Vaca	17. Amerigo Vespucci
23. Magellan	20. Rapids
25. Indian	21. Raleigh
26. East	22. Coronado
28. Narvaez	24. Line

(Across, cont.)		(Down, cont.)	
30.	Drake	27.	Trade
32.	Hudson	29.	Weymouth
33.	Fish	30.	De Soto
34.	Rivers	31.	Marquette
37.	Cabot	35.	Quebec
40.	La Salle	36.	Joliet
41.	Frobisher	38.	Balboa
43.	Trapper	39.	Canoe
44.	Ponce de Leon	41.	Fur
		42.	Spain

Land Ho!

1. Italian
   Discovery of America, 1492, landed in West Indies
   Santa Maria, Niña, Pinta
2. Italian
   Laid claim to the Nova Scotia area for England, discovered the Grand Banks
   England
   His son, Sebastian
3. Spanish
   Sailed to Venezuela, 1499
   Christopher Columbus
4. Portuguese
   Discovered Brazil in 1500
   India (It is believed he had secret orders to sail west to the New World)
5. English
   First Englishman and second European to sail around the world
   Golden Hind
   Spain (Spanish Armada in 1588)
6. Norse
   First European to reach America, A.D. 1000
   Greenland
7. English
   Explored New England coast in 1602, giving Cape Cod the name it bears
   Jamestown

8. English
   Discovered Hudson River and Hudson Bay in 1609 and 1610
   He, several crew members, and his son were set adrift in
   Hudson Bay, never to be heard of again.
   England and Holland
   Hudson River and Hudson Bay

9. Portuguese
   1519 to 1522, was first to sail around the world
   None, he was killed by the natives in the Philippines.

10. Spanish
    Discovered the Pacific Ocean, 1513
    A stowaway

11. French
    Explored the lower Mississippi Valley, 1698 to 1720
    New Orleans

12. Spanish
    Explored the Gulf Plain from Florida to Mexico, 1527 to 1536
    American buffalo (bison)

13. French
    Explored the St. Lawrence River, 1603 to 1615
    Quebec
    New York and Vermont

14. Spanish
    Explored the southwestern United States, 1540 to 1542
    Seven Cities of Gold

15. Spanish
    Conquered Mexico, 1519 to 1521
    The horse

16. Spanish
    Discovered the Mississippi River in 1540
    He was buried in the Mississippi River to prevent the Indians
    from learning of his death.

17. French
    Explored the Upper Mississippi, 1672 to 1673
    Father Marquette
    Trapper

18. French
    Sailed on the Mississippi, laying claim for France, 1684 to

1685
Niagara Falls
19. Spanish
Discovered and named Florida in 1513
The Fountain of Youth
20. Italian
America was named for him
On a map showing the New World he scrawled his name across the newly discovered land.

The War of the Revolution

I	O	T	V	U	E	L	R	N	O
1	2	3	4	5	6	7	8	9	10

spells Revolution

Men of the Revolution

1. Hale
2. Henry
3. Burgoyne
4. Arnold
5. Jefferson
6. Morris

Underlined letters spell heroes.

Revolutionary Quickie

1. Howe
2. Arnold
3. Madison
4. Intolerable
5. Lexington
6. Tory
7. Otis
8. Navigation

First letters spell Hamilton.

America's Lasting Constitution

1.	B	11.	D	1.	T	11.	F
2.	A	12.	C	2.	T	12.	T
3.	D	13.	B	3.	T	13.	F
4.	B	14.	D	4.	F	14.	F
5.	C	15.	C	5.	T	15.	F
6.	A	16.	C	6.	F	16.	F
7.	A	17.	C	7.	T	17.	F
8.	C	18.	C	8.	T	18.	F
9.	A	19.	C	9.	T	19.	F
10.	C	20.	A	10.	T	20.	F

The War of 1812

$$\frac{C}{1} \frac{O}{2} \frac{N}{3} \frac{S}{4} \frac{T}{5} \frac{I}{6} \frac{T}{7} \frac{U}{8} \frac{T}{9} \frac{I}{10} \frac{O}{11} \frac{N}{12}$$

North and South in Conflict

$$\frac{C}{1} \frac{O}{2} \frac{N}{3} \frac{F}{4} \frac{E}{5} \frac{D}{6} \frac{E}{7} \frac{R}{8} \frac{A}{9} \frac{T}{10} \frac{E}{11}$$

Civil War Quickie

1. Longstreet
2. Illinois
3. North
4. Clay
5. Ord
6. Lee
7. Negroes

The first letters spell Lincoln.

Civil Cross-Up

Across	Down
2. Hill	1. Jackson
5. Burnside	3. Longstreet
7. Johnston	4. McDowell
8. Sickles	6. McClellan
9. Sheridan	9. Stuart
11. Pope	10. Anderson
12. Beauregard	11. Porter
15. Lee	13. Grant
16. Mac	14. Ewell
17. Troops	18. Rosecrans
20. Hill	19. Sherman
23. Buell	21. Forrest
24. Custer	22. Ashby
26. Meade	23. Bragg
27. Early	25. Smith
28. Hampton	

America's Territorial Growth

1. Louisiana   Colorado   Minnesota
   Arkansas   Kansas   North Dakota
   Oklahoma   Nebraska   South Dakota
   Missouri   Iowa   Montana
                Wyoming

2. Louisiana
3. Mississippi   Alabama
4. North Dakota   South Dakota   Minnesota
5. Florida
6. Texas   New Mexico   Wyoming
    Oklahoma   Colorado   Kansas
7. Washington   Idaho   Wyoming
    Oregon   Montana
8. California   Arizona   Colorado
    Nevada   Utah   Wyoming
    New Mexico
9. Arizona   New Mexico
10. Alaska
11. Hawaii

The Growth of the Union

Delaware (1787)
Massachusetts (1788)
North Carolina (1789)
Rhode Island (1790)
Vermont (1791)
Tennessee (1796)
Ohio (1803)
Illinois (1818)
Maine (1820)
Missouri (1821)

Florida (1845)
California (1850)
West Virginia (1863)
Colorado (1876)
Montana (1889)
Utah (1896)
Oklahoma (1907)
Arizona (1912)
Alaska (1959)
Hawaii (1959)

America's First Citizens

1. Powhatan
2. Pocahontas
3. Squanto
4. King Philip
5. Pontiac
6. Sitting Bull
7. Sacajawea
8. Tecumseh
9. Ouray
10. Geronimo
11. Cochise
12. Logan
13. Billy Bowlegs
14. Osceola
15. Chief Joseph
16. Opechancanough
17. Little Turtle
18. Weatherford
19. Black Hawk
20. Wildcat

The Wildest of the West

1. Pat Garrett
2. Bat Masterson
3. Wyatt Earp
4. Wild Bill Hickok
5. Bill Tilghman
6. Jim Bridger

7.	Daniel Boone	10.	Jedediah Smith	13.	Jesse James
8.	James Bowie	11.	William Cody	14.	Bob Dalton
9.	Kit Carson	12.	Calamity Jane	15.	William Quantrill

Beginnings

1. The Ku Klux Klan
2. Nickel (It was mostly copper and not to exceed twenty-five percent nickel.)
3. The American Society for the Prevention of Cruelty to Animals
4. The cigarette
5. Prohibition Party
6. Montgomery Ward
7. Democratic Party (Thomas Nast in *Harper's* in 1874 completed the symbols with the elephant for the Republican Party.)
8. Nineteenth Amendment adopted in 1919
9. New Haven, Connecticut
10. Frank W. Woolworth
11. Clara Barton
12. Dorothy Dix
13. The first great oil strike in Texas
14. The "Great Train Robbery"
15. Teddy Roosevelt
16. Orville and Wilbur Wright
17. Industrial Workers of the World
18. Mutual Broadcasting
    American Broadcasting Company (ABC)
    National Broadcasting Company (NBC)
    Columbia Broadcasting System (CBS)
19. National Association for the Advancement of Colored People
20. Henry Ford

Headlines

1. Lincoln
   Ford's
2. *Sultana*
3. Thirteenth
4. *Great Eastern*
5. Johnson
   Secretary of War
6. Johnson

7.	Eight	22.	*Maine*
8.	Fourteenth		Havana
9.	Railroad	23.	United States
	Utah	24.	Spain
10.	Wyoming	25.	United States
11.	Negroes		Spain
12.	Little Big Horn	26.	Galveston
	Sitting Bull	27.	Platt
13.	Garfield	28.	McKinley
	Charles Guiteau		Pan American Exposition
14.	Cleveland	29.	McKinley
	Bedloe	30.	Panama Canal
	France	31.	Theodore Roosevelt
	One hundred		Panama
15.	Pennsylvania		Panamanian
	Dam	32.	Panamanian
	Water	33.	Russia
16.	Sherman		Japan
17.	McKinley Tariff Act	34.	Did
	Highest	35.	Pure Food and Drug Act
18.	Circuit Court of Appeals	36.	Taft
19.	Plessy		The federal income tax
	Equal	37.	*Titanic*
20.	Klondike		Iceberg
	Dawson	38.	Theodore Roosevelt
	Canada		Republican
21.	Spanish		Progressive
	Hearst	39.	Senators
	William McKinley	40.	Panama

The Melting Pot

1.	Italian	Atomic physicist—Nobel Prize winner
2.	German	Baseball player
3.	Jewish	Entertainer
4.	Polish	Musician
5.	Greek	President of Twentieth Century-Fox
6.	Scottish	Senator
7.	Italian	Boxer
8.	Russian	Choreographer

9.	French	Married John Alden (name is really Molines)
10.	English	Labor organizer
11.	Swedish	Poet
12.	Italian	Baseball player
13.	Peruvian	Entertainer
14.	Dutch	Revolutionary War general
15.	Polish	Baseball player
16.	Scottish	Naval hero
17.	Irish	Playwright
18.	Italian	Politician (Mayor of New York City)
19.	Dutch	Railroad magnate
20.	Swedish	Inventor (*Monitor*)
21.	Argentinean	Entertainer
22.	Dutch	Playwright
23.	Polish	Musician (drummer)
24.	Irish	President
25.	Jewish	Polio vaccine
26.	German	Revolutionary War general
27.	Irish	Boxer
28.	French	Aided Colonists in Revolution
29.	Swedish	Aviator
30.	Jewish	Physicist (Nobel Prize winner)

Headliners of the '20's and a Bit Before

Sports: Dempsey over Willard, July 4, 1919
      Grange with Bears, November 26, 1925
      Tunney over Dempsey, September 23, 1926
      Ruth hits sixty homers, 1927

Travel: NC-4, May 16-17, 1919
      Lindbergh, May 20-21, 1927
      Model A, December 2, 1927

The "Twenties" in High Places:
      Harding becomes President, March 4, 1921
      Teapot Dome, April 7, 1922
      Elk Hills, December 11, 1922
      Harding dies, August 2, 1923

Crime and Court:
      Palmer raids, January 1, 1920
      Sacco and Vanzetti, April 15, 1920

House of Morgan, September 16, 1920
Hall-Mills, September 16, 1922
Bobby Franks, May 22, 1924
Scopes Trial, July 24, 1925
Rothstein, November 6, 1928
St. Valentine's Massacre, February 14, 1929
Documents of the "Jazz Era":
Armistice, November 11, 1918
Prohibition Amendment, January 16, 1919
Women get the vote, August 26, 1920
"Arms Parley," November 12, 1921
Boom to Bust:
Coolidge, August 2, 1923
Hoover, March 4, 1929
Black Friday, October 29, 1929
Never Befores:
Boston Police, September 9, 1919
KDKA, November 2, 1920
Beauty contest, September, 1921
Coué, Early in 1923
Floyd Collins, February 17, 1925

World War II Dictionary
1. Torpedo
2. Lightning war
3. Situation normal—all fouled up
4. Sitting war
5. G.P. (General purpose car)
6. Atomic bomb
7. General issue
8. Junior grade
9. Kitchen police
10. Battleship
11. Artificial harbor built for use at Normandy
12. C-47
13. Landing Ship, Tank
14. German hand grenade
15. B-17
16. Japanese suicide plane used in the later days of the Pacific War

17. Traitor (Vidkun Quisling of Norway)
18. Northern Burma to Southwestern China over the Himalaya Mountains
19. Skipping Pacific Islands but cutting off Japanese supply lines, forcing Japanese withdrawal or weakening
20. V-1 German rocket propelled glider bomb
21. Victory in Japan
22. Gas saving measure where members of the group provided transportation in rotation for others in the group
23. Victory in Europe (Germany)
24. Aircraft carrier
25. Depth charges
26. Route of Japanese supply line between Japan and Guadalcanal
27. Groups of submarines
28. Device used on American destroyer escorts to spread depth charges in wide patterns
29. Tinfoil strips used to foul German radar equipment during the Normandy landings
30. Battleship *Missouri* on which the Japanese surrender was signed

World War II Nicknames
1. Field Marshal Sir Bernard Montgomery
2. Dwight David Eisenhower
3. George Patton, Jr.
4. Sir Winston Churchill
5. Joseph Stilwell
6. Douglas MacArthur
7. Field Marshal Erwin Rommel
8. Jonathan M. Wainwright
9. William F. Halsey
10. Benito Mussolini
11. Henry Harley Arnold
12. William Joyce (British traitor)
13. Adolf Hitler
14. Iva Toguri D'Aquino
15. Cordell Hull
16. Joseph Stalin
17. Haile Selassie

18. Franklin D. Roosevelt
19. Mrs. Winston Churchill (Clementine)
20. Gregory Boyington (Pacific Air Ace)

Ships as Makers of History

1.	W	6.	G	11.	J	16.	Q	21.	I
2.	B	7.	O	12.	P	17.	N	22.	D
3.	K	8.	A	13.	V	18.	R	23.	C
4.	W	9.	S	14.	T	19.	M	24.	E
5.	L	10.	U	15.	W	20.	H	25.	F

America, a Land of Connections
1. Pony Express
2. Erie Canal
3. Panama Canal
4. Braddock's Road
5. Old National Road
6. Welland Ship Canal

7. Illinois and Michigan Canal
8. Oregon Trail
9. Missouri Pacific Railroad
10. New York Central Company

11. Santa Fé Trail
12. Mormon Trail
13. Alcan Highway
14. Oregon Trail
15. Transatlantic Cable
16. Pennsylvania Portage and Canal system
17. Cumberland Road
18. Potomac Canal
19. George Washington Bridge
20. St. Lawrence Seaway

North, South, East, and West
1. West
2. East West
3. Southwest
4. West
5. Northwest
6. West
7. South
8. West
9. North South
10. Northwest
11. Northern
12. East
13. West
14. East
15. Southern
16. South
17. West
18. North
19. North
20. East West

Colleges and Universities of America
1. Princeton University—Princeton, New Jersey
2. University of Pennsylvania—Philadelphia, Pennsylvania

3. Harvard University—Cambridge, Massachusetts
4. Oberlin College—Oberlin, Ohio
5. Washington and Lee University—Lexington, Virginia
6. William and Mary College—Williamsburg, Virginia
7. Antioch College—Yellow Springs, Ohio
8. United States Military Academy—West Point, New York
9. Columbia University—New York, New York
10. United States Naval Academy—Annapolis, Maryland

Man, the Builder

1. Empire State Building
2. Hoover Dam
3. Washington Monument
4. Verrazano-Narrows Bridge
5. U.S.S. *United States*
6. Yerkes Observatory—Williams Bay, Wisconsin
7. Mount Rushmore
8. Statue of Liberty
9. Panama Canal
10. Alaska Highway (Alcan Highway)
11. St. Lawrence Seaway
12. Royal Gorge Suspension Bridge
13. The Pentagon
14. KXGO-TV Tower
15. Mount Palomar Observatory, California
16. U.S.S. *Enterprise*
17. Lake Mead
18. University of Michigan at Ann Arbor
19. Chicago—O'Hare International Airport
20. San Jacinto Monument

Inventors and Their Inventions

1. R	6. X	11. P	16. E or F	21. U or T
2. M	7. O	12. G	17. F or E	22. L
3. W	8. N	13. B	18. J	23. D
4. Q	9. A or C	14. Y	19. H	24. I
5. K	10. C or A	15. V	20. T or U	25. S

Was History Like This?

1. Pilgrims
2. He heard the Yankees were playing.

3. Columbus
4. He knew all the verses of the "Star-Spangled Banner."
5. Because he is the national him
6. When he took a hack at the cherry tree
7. Baby bald eagles
8. At the bottom
9. An ex pres
10. So he could have a Gettysburg address

History in Code

1. "The only thing we have to fear is fear itself."　F. D. Roosevelt

2. "Four score and seven years ago our fathers brought forth on this continent . . . ."　A. Lincoln

3. "We the people of the United States . . . ."　Constitution

4. "When in the course of human events . . . ."　Declaration of Independence

5. "One if by land, and two if by sea."　Longfellow

Mightier Than the Sword

1. Benjamin Harris	7. Henry George
2. Benjamin Franklin	8. Edward Bellamy
3. Thomas Paine	9. Frederick Jackson Turner
4. Thomas Jefferson, John Adams, Benjamin Franklin	10. Theodore Dreiser
	11. Frank Norris
	12. Frank Norris
5. Alexander Hamilton, John Jay, James Madison	13. Upton Sinclair
	14. Sinclair Lewis
	15. William Faulkner
6. Harriet Beecher Stowe	16. John Steinbeck

Battle Cryptograms

1. "Don't fire until you see the whites of their eyes." Colonel William Prescott at Bunker Hill

2. "You may fire when ready, Gridley." Commodore George Dewey at Manila Bay

3. "Damn the torpedoes! . . . go ahead." Admiral David Glasgow Farragut in Mobile Bay

4. "Don't give up the ship." Captain James Lawrence aboard the Chesapeake outside Boston Harbor

5. "I have not yet begun to fight." Captain John Paul Jones on *Bonhomme Richard* off Scotland

6. "Hold the fort! I am coming!" William Tecumseh Sherman at Allatoona Pass, Georgia

Quotable Quotes

1. C	9. B	17. B	25. C	33. B
2. B	10. C	18. B	26. A	34. B
3. B	11. B	19. A	27. B	35. A
4. A	12. B	20. C	28. A	36. B
5. B	13. B	21. A	29. B	37. A
6. B	14. C	22. B	30. C	38. B
7. A	15. B	23. A	31. C	39. B
8. B	16. B	24. C	32. A	40. C

America's Religious History

1. Mary Baker Eddy
2. Anne Hutchinson
3. Roger Williams
4. William Penn
5. Brigham Young
6. Marcus Whitman
7. Cotton Mather
8. Billy Sunday
9. Joseph Smith
10. Peter Marshall
11. Norman Vincent Peale
12. Billy Graham
13. Henry Ward Beecher
14. William Jennings Bryan
15. William Brewster
16. Thomas Hooker

Spells Religious Leaders

Military Leaders in Disguise

1. Ewell
2. Grant
3. Lee
4. Patton
5. Putnam
6. Pershing
7. Jackson
8. Marshall
9. Sherman
10. Sheridan
11. Scott
12. Perry
13. Meade
14. Longstreet
15. Arnold
16. Wayne
17. Pope
18. Halsey
19. King
20. Porter

Noted American Homes

1. George Washington
2. Thomas Jefferson
3. Andrew Jackson
4. Patrick Henry
5. C. Vanderbilt
6. Henry Ford
7. George Vanderbilt
8. John Adams
9. Franklin Roosevelt
10. Robert E. Lee

11. Henry Clay
12. Dwight Eisenhower
13. John D. Rockefeller
14. James Madison

15. Calvin Coolidge
16. James Monroe
17. Theodore Roosevelt
18. U.S. Presidents

Biography Detection

A. Hamilton
B. Westinghouse
C. Patton
D. Washington
E. Winston Churchill
F. Cleveland
G. Garfield
H. Fiorello La Guardia

I. Carry Nation
J. Woodrow Wilson
K. (William Randolph) Hearst
L. Chamberlain
M. Farragut
N. William Seward

For Biographers and Such

1. John Paul Jones
2. John Randolph
3. Samuel Houston
4. Jane Addams
5. Horace Greeley
6. Andrew Jackson
7. Oliver Wendell Holmes, Jr.
8. Samuel Gompers
9. Albert Einstein
10. John L. Lewis
11. Clara Barton
12. Stephen A. Douglas
13. Samuel L. Clemens
14. Dwight David Eisenhower

15. John J. Pershing
16. Alexander Graham Bell
17. Clarence Darrow
18. Harry S. Truman
19. Charles Evans Hughes
20. Chester William Nimitz
21. Douglas MacArthur
22. Eleanor Roosevelt
23. George Washington
24. Jeb Stuart
25. John Hancock
26. Ben Franklin
27. John Adams
28. John C. Frémont
29. John Pierpont Morgan
30. Henry Clay

Nicknames of the Great

1. Andrew Jackson
2. Thomas Jackson
3. John C. Frémont
4. William Henry Harrison
5. Martin Van Buren

6. John Quincy Adams
7. Chester A. Arthur
8. Theodore Roosevelt
9. Zachary Taylor
10. William Jennings Bryan

11. Israel Putnam	29. Francis Marion
12. Abraham Lincoln	30. Dwight D. Eisenhower
13. Winfield Scott	31. Samuel Wilson
14. John J. Pershing	32. George B. McClellan
15. George H. Thomas	33. George Washington
16. John Philip Sousa	34. Martin Van Buren
17. George B. McClellan	35. Ulysses S. Grant
18. Elmer Ellsworth	36. Henry Lee (father of
19. Abraham Lincoln	Robert E.)
20. Thomas Jefferson	37. Calvin Coolidge
21. George Armstrong Custer	38. Robert E. Lee
22. William Jennings Bryan	39. Pierre Gustave de Beau-
23. Henry Clay	regard
24. Stephen A. Douglas	40. Cordell Hull
25. Martha Jane Burke	41. Charles A. Lindbergh
26. Lucy Hayes	42. Anthony Wayne
27. Sam Houston	43. Harry S. Truman
28. Samuel L. Clemens	44. James Ewell Brown Stuart

Pairs and Couples

1. Ira Gershwin or Martha Washington

2. Dolley Madison	12. Clark
3. Joliet	13. Serapis
4. Bess Truman	14. Eleanor Roosevelt
5. Monitor	15. Martha Washington or
6. John Alden	Ira Gershwin
7. John Smith or John Rolfe	16. Hammerstein
8. Mamie Eisenhower	17. Kaufman
9. Jacqueline Kennedy	18. Daffy Dean
10. Vanzetti	19. Lewis
11. Loeb	20. Huck Finn

Great Americans and Their Dogs and Horses

Dogs

1. Skip	4. Fala
2. Laddie Boy	5. Him and Her
3. Rob Roy	

Horses

1. Nelson	3. Traveller
2. Old Whitey	4. Little Sorrel

217

5. Truxton   7. Cincinnatus
6. Rienzi

America's Well-Educated Presidents

1. George Washington   Abraham Lincoln
   Andrew Jackson   Andrew Johnson
   Martin Van Buren   Grover Cleveland
   Zachary Taylor   Harry Truman
   Millard Fillmore
2. John Adams   Franklin Roosevelt
   John Quincy Adams   John F. Kennedy
   Theodore Roosevelt
3. Thomas Jefferson   John Tyler
   James Monroe
4. James Madison   Woodrow Wilson
5. Ulysses Grant   Dwight Eisenhower
6. William H. Harrison—   William McKinley—
      Hampden-Sydney   Allegheny
   James Polk—   William Howard Taft—
      North Carolina   Yale
   Franklin Pierce—Bowdoin   Warren Harding—
   James Buchanan—Dickin-   Ohio Central
      son   Calvin Coolidge—Amherst
   Rutherford B. Hayes—   Herbert Hoover—Stanford
      Kenyon   Lyndon B. Johnson—
   James Garfield—Williams   Southwest Texas State
   Chester A. Arthur—Union   College
   Benjamin Harrison—
      Miami

Soldiers in the White House

1. D	5. R	9. O	13. E	17. K
2. M	6. F	10. C	14. I	18. L
3. P	7. Q	11. T	15. A	19. H
4. G	8. S	12. N	16. J	20. B

Wives of the Presidents

1. Bess Truman
   A. Blair House   B. Margaret
   C. United States Senate

2. Jacqueline Kennedy
   - A. languages
   - B. Washington
   - C. college studied University
   - D. Q. Jack
3. Mary Lincoln
   - A. Civil War
   - B. son
   - C. years term
   - D. Proclamation
4. Dolley Madison
   - A. Washington
   - B. years glamorous ladies
   - C. died
5. Eleanor Roosevelt
   - A. United Nations
   - B. governor
   - C. Pearl Harbor
   - D. elected
6. Helen Taft
   - A. Tidal Basin
   - B. Orchestra
   - C. Chief
   - D. General
7. Abigail Adams
   - A. President
   - B. France England
   - C. White House completed
   - D. Marshall husband President
8. Florence Harding
   - A. editor Star
   - B. horse
   - C. Conference
   - D. oil grief
9. Lou Hoover
   - A. engineer
   - B. Scouts
   - C. husband active London
10. Julia Grant
    - A. general
    - B. July royalties
    - C. Drive

Assassination!

Abraham Lincoln	James A. Garfield
Andrew Johnson	Chester A. Arthur
April 14, 1865	July 2, 1881
April 15	September 19
Ford's Theater	Railroad Station
John Wilkes Booth	Charles J. Guiteau
Washington, D.C.	Washington, D.C.

William McKinley	John F. Kennedy
Theodore Roosevelt	Lyndon B. Johnson
September 6, 1901	November 22, 1963
September 14	November 22
Pan-American Exposition	Parade
Leon Czolgosz	Lee Harvey Oswald
Buffalo, New York	Dallas, Texas

Who Was President When . . . ?

1. Franklin D. Roosevelt	10. Dwight D. Eisenhower
2. Grover Cleveland	11. Herbert Hoover
3. Woodrow Wilson	12. Ulysses S. Grant
4. Andrew Johnson	13. James Madison
5. Andrew Jackson	14. George Washington
6. William McKinley	15. James Buchanan
7. Harry S. Truman	16. Theodore Roosevelt
8. Thomas Jefferson	17. Abraham Lincoln
9. James Monroe	

Presidential Cross-Up

Across	Down
2. Van Buren	1. J. Q. Adams
3. Harding	4. Grant
6. Taylor	5. T. Roosevelt
10. Washington	7. Lincoln
11. Fillmore	8. Garfield
12. Hoover	9. B. Harrison
14. Coolidge	10. Wilson
15. Taft	13. Jefferson
16. Monroe	15. Truman
17. J. Adams	19. Eisenhower
18. McKinley	20. W. Harrison
22. Buchanan	21. A. Johnson
25. Pierce	23. Cleveland
26. F. Roosevelt	24. Arthur
28. Madison	27. Jackson
31. Kennedy	29. Hayes
32. Tyler	30. Polk
33. L. Johnson	

Moments from History

1. Haymarket Riot
2. San Francisco
3. Chicago fire
4. League of Nations
5. Progressive
6. Panama
7. Boxer Rebellion
8. Bland-Allison Act
9. Knights of Labor
10. Plessy v. Ferguson
11. New Lands Act
12. Platt Amendment
13. Russo-Japanese War
14. Boy Scouts of America
15. *Lusitania*
16. *Sussex* affair
17. Paratroops
18. Peace Corps
19. Spitfire
20. Lend-lease
21. Zimmermann note

Word Search

1. Arnold
2. Lee
3. Ford
4. Indian
5. A.F.L.-C.I.O.
6. Ironclad
7. Oil
8. Paine
9. Eli
10. Canal
11. Centennial
12. Land
13. California
14. Penn
15. Panic

Second Word Search

1. Marines
2. Trade
3. Adams
4. Canada
5. Asia
6. Census
7. Erie
8. Iron
9. Maine
10. Radio
11. Reed
12. Senate
13. Truman
14. Censor
15. Courts
16. Edison
17. Draft
18. Income
19. Steam
20. Tea
21. Treaties
22. Tories
23. Ute
24. Atomic
25. Scott

Links of History

Across

1. Boston
3. Tory
4. Texas
6. Roger
7. Alamo
8. Hayes
10. Rolfe
12. Lewis
14. Ewell
16. Stuart
18. Mellon
20. Harte
22. Radio
23. Fort
24. Debs
26. Kidd

Down

1. Bunker
2. Native
4. Taylor
5. Slater
8. Hoover
9. Strike
11. Low
12. Lake
13. Sail
15. Latter
16. Salem
17. Train
19. Luther
20. Hitler
21. Eskimo
24. Dunkirk

(Across cont.)		(Down cont.)	
27. Austin	33. Canals	25. Sanford	34. Sumter
28. Patent	36. Teapot	28. Paine	35. Allen
30. Edison	37. Pierce	29. Twain	37. Pitt
32. Sutter	40. Revere	31. Taft	38. East
		33. Custis	39. Vote

Who, What, When, Why, and How?

1. He was not married.
2. The first atomic bomb explosion was July 16, 1945, at Alamogordo, New Mexico. Germany surrendered May 7, 1945.
3. In his famous poem, "Paul Revere's Ride," Henry Wadsworth Longfellow mentions only Paul Revere.
4. Its cornerstone was laid in 1792; and when John and Abigail Adams moved in in 1802, it was still not completed.
5. Geronimo was an Apache.
6. Railroad competition was too much for many of the canals.
7. Jefferson
8. Molly Pitcher
9. Manila Bay
10. San Jacinto, Texas
11. Montgomery, Alabama, and Richmond, Virginia
12. Jefferson Davis
13. Dolley Madison
14. The Barbary pirates
15. None. The U.S. did not exist as a nation at that time.
16. John Hancock
17. It was America's first submarine.
18. It was the first permanent English settlement in America.
19. Tobacco
20. John Rolfe
21. a. Colonists elected representatives to the House of Burgesses, a law-making assembly.
    b. A shipload of women to become wives of the Colonists arrived.
    c. The first Negro slaves to arrive in America were sold in Jamestown.
22. Victoria, the only one of Magellan's five ships to complete the voyage
23. The first ten amendments to the Constitution

222

24. Betsy Ross of Philadelphia
25. The Boston Tea Party of 1773 protested the English tax on tea.
26. Harriet Beecher Stowe
27. Andrew Johnson
28. Theodore Roosevelt
29. Franklin Roosevelt
30. "The Star-Spangled Banner"
31. Peter Stuyvesant
32. Andrew Jackson
33. Union Pacific
34. The Black Hawk War in 1832
35. The Panama Canal
36. Henry Clay—1824, 1832, 1844
    William Jennings Bryan—1896, 1900, 1908
37. The underground railroad
38. Nathan Hale
39. Horace Greeley
40. Barbara Frietchie
41. Harvard was founded in 1636.
42. Theodore Roosevelt
43. Spanish American War, 1898
44. She with five others was involved with John Wilkes Booth in the Lincoln assassination plot.
45. The *Alabama*
46. The Virgin Islands
47. Belle Boyd
48. Rose Greenhow
49. James Bowie invented the Bowie knife.
50. Priscilla Mullins
51. *Flying Cloud*
52. John Peter Zenger
53. Julia Ward Howe
54. The Overland Trail
55. Peggy Shippen, young wife of Benedict Arnold
56. Clara Barton
57. Booker T. Washington
58. John Paul Jones
59. Benjamin Franklin

60. The *Monitor*
61. Caesar Rodney
62. John Calhoun resigned when Andrew Jackson was President of the U.S.
63. Roanoke Island, North Carolina, August 18, 1587
64. St. Augustine, Florida, 1565, founded by the Spanish
65. It was squeezing the life out of the South by stopping the trade with the rest of the world.
66. Johnny Appleseed planted apple seeds over thousands of square miles in the Ohio River Valley between 1800 and 1848.
67. Andrew Jackson, although leading in the number of electoral votes, lost the election to John Q. Adams when the election was decided in the House of Representatives.
68. Revolutionary War, April 19, 1775
    Civil War, April 12, 1861
    Spanish American War, April 25, 1898
    World War I, April 6, 1917
69. Jefferson Davis
70. Warren G. Harding
71. Louisiana Purchase from Napoleon for fifteen million dollars in 1803.
72. Ethan Allen
73. He was military governor during the reconstruction of Tennessee.
74. Battle of Manila Bay, May 1, 1898, Spanish American War
75. The War of 1812 had ended before the Battle of New Orleans was fought.

History in Error
1. Paul never reached Concord. He was captured by the British.
2. De Soto was buried in the Mississippi River.
3. The *Bismark* was brought to its end by British warships and torpedo planes. The United States was not in the war at that time.
4. Several air tragedies had previously caused a greater loss of life: The R-38 in 1921 cost sixty-two lives, the Dixmude in 1923 took fifty-two lives, the R-101 took a toll of forty-seven in 1930, the Akron in 1933 killed seventy-two, and the Maxim Gorkey crashed killing forty-nine in 1935.

5. Actually, the Proclamation only freed those slaves in areas still in rebellion against the United States. Of course, these slaves were not actually freed until the Union had defeated the Confederacy and could force the issue.

6. Burr killed Hamilton.

7. Custer was a general at the time.

8. Lincoln died in 1865, and negotiations began in December, 1866, with the treaty being signed in 1867. President Andrew Johnson was President of the United States at the time.

9. Seaboard Airline is a railroad.

10. Roosevelt and his men advanced on foot, despite the famous painting which portrays them riding forward.

11. The Pilgrims were relative latecomers to New England. To name a few, Sir John Popham, Sir Ferdinando Gorges, Captain John Smith, and Richard Vines had all explored along the New England coast before the coming of the Pilgrims. And of course the Cabot explorations shouldn't be forgotten, nor those of Hudson and Champlain.

12. V-2's first landed in London on September 12, 1944, and continued to bring destruction until their launching pads were captured by the advancing Allied armies in the closing days of the war.

13. The RFC (Reconstruction Finance Corporation) was a measure sponsored by Hoover which was established on February 2, 1932.

14. This famous battle was fought after the Treaty of Ghent had been signed, officially ending the war on December 24, 1814.

15. General George S. Patton, Jr., was "the general in spurs."

16. One driver stayed in America instead of returning home. He was Hadji Ali.

17. Lee's horse was named Traveller.

18. Peary reached the North Pole.

Answers to Geographical Quizzes

Hidden States

1. Alaska	6. Missouri	11. Iowa	16. Montana
2. Wash-ington	7. Oregon	12. Alabama	17. Vermont
		13. Utah	18. Maryland
3. Indiana	8. Idaho	14. Nevada	19. Florida
4. Texas	9. Colorado	15. Delaware	20. Ohio
5. Maine	10. Kentucky		

The Naming of the States

1. Colorado	8. Vermont	15. Pennsylvania
2. Maine	9. Wyoming	16. Kansas
3. Maryland	10. Indiana	17. Mississippi
4. Washington	11. Delaware	18. Wisconsin
5. Alaska	12. Florida	19. Iowa
6. Montana	13. Georgia	20. Oklahoma
7. Nevada	14. New York	

Now for Nicknames

1. Arkansas—Land of Opportunity
2. Missouri—Show Me State
3. Texas—Lone Star State
4. Oregon—Beaver State

5. New Hampshire—Granite State
6. Rhode Island—Little Rhody
7. Wyoming—Equality State
8. Mississippi—Magnolia State
9. Arizona—Grand Canyon State
10. Hawaii—Aloha State
11. Kentucky—Blue Grass State
12. Michigan—Wolverine State
13. New Mexico—Land of Enchantment
14. West Virginia—Mountain State
15. Montana—Treasure State
16. Ohio—Buckeye State
17. South Carolina—Palmetto State
18. Pennsylvania—Keystone State
19. Utah—Beehive State
20. Illinois—Prairie State
21. Louisiana—Pelican State
22. Iowa—Hawkeye State
23. Maine—Pine Tree State
24. Alabama—Heart of Dixie, Cotton State
25. Alaska—Land of the Midnight Sun
26. Massachusetts—Old Colony, Bay State
27. Minnesota—Gopher State, North Star State
28. Florida—Sunshine State
29. Wisconsin—Badger State
30. Oklahoma—Sooner State
31. South Dakota—Coyote State, Sunshine State
32. Tennessee—Volunteer State
33. Nebraska—Cornhusker State
34. Virginia—Old Dominion
35. Idaho—Gem State
36. Colorado—Centennial State
37. Delaware—First State, Diamond State
38. Kansas—Sunflower State
39. Nevada—Silver State
40. New Jersey—Garden State
41. Washington—Evergreen State
42. North Dakota—Sioux State, Flickertail State
43. North Carolina—Tar Heel State

44. California—Golden State
45. Georgia—Empire State of the South
46. Connecticut—Constitution State
47. Maryland—Free State, Old Line State
48. Vermont—Green Mountain State
49. New York—Empire State
50. Indiana—Hoosier State

In and Around America's Great Cities

1. Denver	5. Chicago	9. Washington,
2. San Francisco	6. Boston	D.C.
3. New York	7. Philadelphia	10. Richmond
4. New Orleans	8. Los Angeles	

Where in the World?

1. Texas	12. South Dakota	23. Washington
2. California	13. Alaska	24. Wyoming
3. New York	14. Hawaii	25. Wyoming
4. Maryland	15. Colorado	26. Texas
5. Colorado	16. Vermont	27. South Dakota
6. Missouri	17. Georgia (Fla.)	28. Virginia
7. New Mexico	18. Utah	29. Massachusetts
8. Arizona	19. California	30. California
9. Arizona	20. California	31. New York
10. Pennsylvania	21. California	32. Kentucky
11. Massachusetts	22. Oregon	

A Capital Scramble

1. Alabama	5. Georgia	9. Ohio
2. Washington	6. Indiana	10. Tennessee
3. Hawaii	7. Nevada	
4. South Carolina	8. New Mexico	

The scrambled first letters spell Washington.

States and Capitals Criss-Cross

Across	Down
2. North Carolina	1. Louisiana
4. Mississippi	3. Michigan
5. Kentucky	6. Nevada

(Across cont.)		(Down cont.)	
7.	West Virginia	8.	Georgia
10.	South Dakota	9.	New Hampshire
11.	Vermont	10.	South Carolina
14.	Hawaii	12.	Maine
17.	Oregon	13.	Tennessee
18.	Alaska	15.	Alabama
19.	Wyoming	16.	Idaho
21.	Oklahoma	17.	Ohio
22.	Delaware	20.	Minnesota
24.	Arizona	23.	New York
29.	Wisconsin	25.	Rhode Island
30.	New Jersey	26.	New Mexico
35.	Texas	27.	Missouri
36.	Arkansas	28.	Pennsylvania
39.	California	31.	Washington
41.	Illinois	32.	Utah
43.	North Dakota	33.	Indiana
45.	Maryland	34.	Virginia
46.	Montana	37.	Nebraska
47.	Connecticut	38.	Colorado
48.	Massachusetts	40.	Florida
		42.	Iowa
		44.	Kansas

Coast to Coast and Border to Border

1. Alaska, Washington, Idaho, Montana, North Dakota, Minnesota, Michigan, Ohio, Pennsylvania, New York, Vermont, New Hampshire, and Maine
2. California, Arizona, New Mexico, and Texas
3. Texas, Louisiana, Mississippi, Alabama, and Florida
4. Washington, Oregon, California, Alaska, and Hawaii
5. Maine, New Hampshire, Massachusetts, Rhode Island, Connecticut, New York, New Jersey, Pennsylvania, Delaware, Maryland, Virginia, North Carolina, South Carolina, Georgia, and Florida

229

Next Door Neighbors
Part I

Wyoming

1. Montana
2. South Dakota
3. Nebraska
4. Colorado
5. Utah
6. Idaho

Alabama

1. Tennessee
2. Georgia
3. Florida
4. Mississippi

Nevada

1. Oregon
2. Idaho
3. Utah
4. Arizona
5. California

Tennessee

1. Kentucky
2. Virginia
3. North Carolina
4. Georgia
5. Alabama
6. Mississippi
7. Arkansas
8. Missouri

Pennsylvania

1. New York
2. New Jersey
3. Delaware
4. Maryland
5. West Virginia
6. Ohio

Oklahoma

1. Kansas
2. Missouri
3. Arkansas
4. Texas
5. New Mexico
6. Colorado

West Virginia

1. Pennsylvania
2. Maryland
3. Virginia
4. Kentucky
5. Ohio

Wisconsin

1. Michigan
2. Illinois
3. Iowa
4. Minnesota

Massachusetts

1. Vermont
2. New Hampshire
3. Rhode Island
4. Connecticut
5. New York

Missouri

1. Iowa
2. Illinois
3. Kentucky
4. Tennessee
5. Arkansas
6. Oklahoma
7. Kansas
8. Nebraska

230

Part II

1. Washington	5. North Carolina	9. North Dakota
2. Maine	6. Louisiana	10. Hawaii or Alaska
3. Florida	7. Arizona	11. Alaska or Hawaii
4. New York	8. Indiana	

Points of the Compass

1. Cheyenne, Wyoming
2. Great Salt Lake
3. Mt. McKinley
4. Houston, Texas
5. Lake Michigan
6. Cape Hatteras
7. Kansas City, Kansas, or Kansas City, Missouri
8. Miami, Florida
9. Yellowstone National Park
10. Buffalo, New York
11. Indianapolis, Indiana
12. Omaha, Nebraska
13. San Diego, California
14. Santa Fe, New Mexico
15. Atlanta, Georgia
16. Honolulu, Hawaii
17. Grand Canyon National Park
18. Detroit, Michigan
19. Jackson, Mississippi
20. Minneapolis, Minnesota
21. Dallas, Texas
22. Annapolis, Maryland
23. Chicago, Illinois
24. Lake Champlain
25. Bismark, North Dakota

It's a Big Country

1. Phoenix, Arizona
2. Reno, Nevada
3. Portland, Oregon
4. Des Moines, Iowa
5. Chicago, Illinois
6. Jackson, Mississippi
7. Cheyenne, Wyoming
8. Boise, Idaho
9. Little Rock, Arkansas
10. Grand Rapids, Michigan
11. Columbia, South Carolina
12. Philadelphia, Pennsylvania
13. Peoria, Illinois
14. Washington, D.C.
15. Omaha, Nebraska
16. Washington, D.C.
17. Atlanta, Georgia
18. Nashville, Tennessee
19. Cleveland, Ohio
20. St. Louis, Missouri

Faraway Places

1. 3,050	6. 1,200	11. 950	16. 1,275
2. 350	7. 250	12. 1,300	17. 400
3. 600	8. 2,100	13. 1,225	18. 750
4. 1,250	9. 400	14. 250	19. 350
5. 1,000	10. 170	15. 800	20. 1,800

231

America, a Land of Great Rivers

1.	Arkansas River	11.	Yazoo River
2.	Hudson River	12.	Susquehanna River
3.	Missouri River	13.	Suwannee River
4.	Mississippi River	14.	Rappahannock River
5.	Rio Grande	15.	Platte River
6.	Colorado River	16.	Wabash River
7.	Columbia River	17.	Ohio River
8.	Delaware River	18.	Potomac River
9.	James River	19.	Snake River
10.	Pecos River	20.	Yukon River

States and Their River Namesakes
1. Colorado, Utah, Arizona, Nevada, California, and Texas
2. Alabama
3. Colorado, Kansas, Oklahoma, and Arkansas
4. Connecticut, Massachusetts, Vermont, and New Hampshire
5. Delaware, New Jersey, New York, Pennsylvania, and Kansas
6. Illinois, Arkansas, Oklahoma, and Oregon
7. Iowa
8. Kansas
9. Kentucky
10. Minnesota
11. Minnesota, Wisconsin, Iowa, Illinois, Missouri, Kentucky, Tennessee, Arkansas, Mississippi, and Louisiana
12. Montana, North Dakota, South Dakota, Nebraska, Iowa, Missouri, and Kansas
13. Kentucky, Illinois, Indiana, Ohio, West Virginia, and Pennsylvania
14. Tennessee, Mississippi, Alabama, and Kentucky
15. Wisconsin

The Colorful United States

1.	Louisiana	6.	Louisiana
2.	Colorado	7.	Colorado
3.	South Dakota	8.	Oregon, Pennsylvania,
4.	Arizona and Oklahoma		Texas, and Washington
5.	Arizona	9.	Utah

232

10. Wisconsin and Michigan
11. Vermont and Wyoming
12. North Carolina
13. Utah
14. Utah
15. Mississippi

16. Indiana, Nebraska, and Oregon
17. New Hampshire
18. Kentucky
19. Tennessee

Colored Rivers
1. Arizona
   Arkansas
   Louisiana
   Maine

   Michigan
   Missouri
   New Jersey
   New York

   North Carolina
   South Carolina
   Vermont
   Wisconsin

2. Indiana

   Missouri

   Oklahoma

3. Vermont

4. Colorado
   Illinois

   Kentucky
   Utah
   Vermont

   Washington
   Wyoming

5. Arkansas
   Kentucky

   Louisiana
   Oklahoma
   Tennessee

   Texas
   Wisconsin

6. Arizona
   Arkansas
   Colorado
   Indiana

   Michigan
   Missouri
   Nebraska
   Nevada
   South Dakota

   Texas
   Utah
   Vermont
   Washington

7. Florida

   Georgia
   Wisconsin

   Indiana

Index of Titles

Index of Subjects